ACTIVITY WORKBOOK

SIDE by SIDE

4 Extra

Steven J. Molinsky
Bill Bliss

with
Carolyn Graham

Contributing Authors
Jennifer Bixby • Elizabeth Handley • Dorothy Lynde

Illustrated by
Richard E. Hill

Side by Side Extra Activity Workbook 4

Pearson Education, 10 Bank Street, White Plains, NY 10606

Staff credits: The people who make up the *Side by Side Extra* team, representing content creation, design, manufacturing, marketing, multimedia, project management, publishing, rights management, and testing are Pietro Alongi, Allen Ascher, Rhea Banker, Elizabeth Barker, Lisa Bayrasli, Elizabeth Carlson, Jennifer Castro, Tracey Munz Cataldo, Diane Cipollone, Aerin Csigay, Victoria Denkus, Dave Dickey, Daniel Dwyer, Wanda España, Oliva Fernandez, Warren Fischbach, Pam Fishman, Nancy Flaggman, Patrice Fraccio, Irene Frankel, Aliza Greenblatt, Lester Holmes, Leslie Johnson, Janet Johnston, Caroline Kasterine, Barry Katzen, Ray Keating, Renee Langan, Jaime Lieber, José Antonio Méndez, Julie Molnar, Alison Pei, Pamela Pia, Stuart Radcliffe, Jennifer Raspiller, Kriston Reinmuth, Mary Perrotta Rich, Tania Saiz-Sousa, Katherine Sullivan, Paula Van Ells, Kenneth Volcjak, Paula Williams, and Wendy Wolf.

Text composition: TSI Graphics, Inc.

Illustrations: Richard E. Hill

The authors gratefully acknowledge the contribution of Tina Carver in the development of the original *Side by Side* program.

ISBN-10: 0-13-245991-4
ISBN-13: 978-0-13-245991-4

Printed in the United States of America

2   17

CONTENTS

STUDENT BOOK
PAGES **1–14**

draw	fly	ride	speak	take
drive	grow	sing	swim	write

1. My son Timmy ___swims___ very well.

   ___He's swum___ for many years.

3. Harry _____ a truck. _____

   _____ a truck for many years.

5. My wife and I _____ in a choir.

   _____ in a choir for many years.

7. Abigail _____ her bicycle to work.

   _____ it to work for many years.

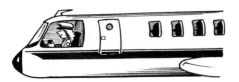

9. Fran _____ airplanes for

   Trans-Globe Airlines. _____

   _____ airplanes for
   Trans-Globe Airlines for many years.

2. Rita _____ guitar lessons. _____

   _____ lessons for many years.

Ciao!

4. I _____ Italian. _____

   _____ Italian for many years.

6. Glen _____ poetry. _____

   _____ poetry for many years.

8. Dave _____ cartoons. _____

   _____ cartoons for many years.

10. My grandfather _____ beautiful

   flowers in his garden. _____

   _____ beautiful flowers in his
   garden for many years.

B A LITTLE WHILE AGO

do	eat	feed	give	go	see	take	write

1. A. ___Have___ the employees ___gone___ on strike yet?

   B. Yes, ___they have___. ___They went___ on strike a little while ago.

2. A. _____ Alice _____ a break yet?

   B. Yes, _____. _____ a break a little while ago.

3. A. _____ you _____ your homework yet?

   B. Yes, _____. _____ it a little while ago.

4. A. _____ you and Susie _____ breakfast yet?

   B. Yes, _____. _____ breakfast a little while ago.

5. A. _____ Frank _____ out the paychecks yet?

   B. Yes, _____. _____ them out a little while ago.

6. A. _____ Monica _____ her report yet?

   B. Yes, _____. _____ it a little while ago.

7. A. _____ you _____ the cats yet?

   B. Yes, _____. _____ them a little while ago.

8. A. _____ Thomas _____ his new son yet?

   B. Yes, _____. _____ him a little while ago.

C LISTENING 🔊

Listen and decide what is being talked about.

1. (a.) songs
   b. clothes

2. a. a horse
   b. a letter

3. a. a language
   b. a book

4. a. a concert hall
   b. a lake

5. a. e-mail
   b. my new bicycle

6. a. cartoons
   b. newspaper articles

7. a. a movie
   b. inventory

8. a. a van
   b. a letter

9. a. friends
   b. flowers

be	do	eat	get	give	go	ride	see	swim	take	write

1. A. ____Have____ you and your husband ____taken____ a walk on the beach recently?

   B. No, ____we haven't____. _____We haven't taken_____ a walk on the beach in a long time.

2. A. _____ Emily _____ a letter to her grandparents recently?

   B. No, _____. _____ to her grandparents in a long time.

3. A. _____ your husband _____ a raise recently?

   B. No, _____. _____ a raise in a long time.

4. A. _____ you _____ bowling recently?

   B. No, _____. _____ bowling in a long time.

5. A. _____ people _____ in the lake outside of town recently?

   B. No, _____. _____ there in a long time.

6. A. _____ your car _____ at the repair shop recently?

   B. No, _____. _____ at the repair shop in a long time.

7. A. _____ you and your wife _____ a movie recently?

   B. No, _____. _____ a movie in a long time.

8. A. _____ Diane _____ her motorcycle recently?

   B. No, _____. _____ it in a long time.

9. A. _____ you _____ at a nice restaurant recently?

   B. No, _____. _____ at a nice restaurant in a long time.

10. A. _____ George _____ anything interesting recently?

    B. No, _____. _____ anything interesting for a long time.

11. A. _____ I _____ you any difficult tests recently?

    B. No, _____. _____ us a difficult test in a long time.

Listen. Then clap and practice.

A. Have you gone   to the zoo?

B.   Yes,   I have.

I went   to the zoo   last May.

And how about   you?   Have you gone there,   too?

A.   No, I haven't.   I'm going   today.

A. Have you seen   the news?

B.   Yes,   I have.

I saw   the news   at seven.

And how about   you?   Have you seen it,   too?

A.   No, I haven't.   I'll see it   at eleven.

A. Have you done   your laundry?

B.   Yes,   I have.

I did   my laundry   last Sunday.

And how about   you?   Have you done yours,   too?

A.   No, I haven't.   I'll do it   next Monday.

A. Have you taken   your driving test?

B.   Yes,   I have.

I took it   last   November.

And how about   you?   Have you taken it,   too?

A.   No, I haven't.   I'll take it   in September.

F WHAT ARE THEY SAYING?

| be | have | know | own | play | sing | want | work | | since | for |

1. A. How long ___has___ Jonathan ___known___ how to ski?

   B. ___He's known___ how to ski ___for___ the past ten years.

2. A. How long _____ your daughter _____ the measles?

   B. _____ the measles _____ last Friday.

3. A. How long _____ you _____ the violin?

   B. _____ the violin _____ several years.

4. A. How long _____ Mr. and Mrs. Chang _____ their own house?

   B. _____ their own house _____ more than a year.

5. A. How long _____ your brother Tom _____ opera?

   B. _____ opera _____ he moved to Italy last year.

6. A. How long _____ your daughter _____ to be a singer?

   B. _____ to be a singer _____ she was ten years old.

7. A. How long _____ you and Kathy _____ at the mall?

   B. _____ at the mall _____ a few months.

8. A. This lecture is extremely long. How long _____ we _____ here?

   B. _____ here _____ more than two hours.

G LISTENING 🔊

Listen and complete the sentences.

1. ⓐ three years.
   b. last year.

2. a. a long time.
   b. they started high school.

3. a. 1999.
   b. fifteen years.

4. a. 1966.
   b. thirty-five years.

5. a. last weekend.
   b. four days.

6. a. I was a young boy.
   b. several years.

7. a. last spring.
   b. three months.

8. a. I moved here.
   b. the past ten years.

9. a. he moved to Boston.
   b. the past twenty years.

WHAT'S THE QUESTION?

1. <u>How long have</u> you <u>had a toothache</u>?

   I've had a toothache for the past two days.

2. _____ your daughter _____?

   She's wanted to be a teacher since she was a child.

3. _____ your husband _____?

   He's been in the hospital for more than a week.

4. _____ your children _____?

   They've known how to swim since they were young.

5. _____ you and your wife _____?

   We've owned our own home for twenty years.

WRITE ABOUT YOURSELF

1. I know how to _____.

   I've known how to _____ (since/for) _____.

2. I like to _____.

   I've liked to _____ (since/for) _____.

3. I own _____.

   I've owned _____ (since/for) _____.

4. I want to _____.

   I've wanted to _____ (since/for) _____.

5. I have _____.

   I've _____ (since/for) _____.

6. I'm _____.

   I've been _____ (since/for) _____.

Activity Workbook 7

J HOW LONG?

1. A. How long has George been waiting for a taxi?

   B. <u>   He's been waiting for a taxi for   </u>
   half an hour.

2. A. How long has Julie been practicing the piano?

   B. _____
   early this afternoon.

3. A. How long have you been feeling sick?

   B. _____
   the past few days.

4. A. How long have I been talking?

   B. _____
   an hour and fifteen minutes.

5. A. How long have Stacy and Tom been going out?

   B. _____
   last summer.

6. A. How long has your car been making strange noises?

   B. _____
   a few weeks.

7. A. How long have you been doing sit-ups?

   B. _____
   twenty minutes.

8. A. How long has Howard been snoring?

   B. _____
   midnight.

K LISTENING

Listen and choose the correct answer.

1. a. He bought his TV a few weeks ago.
    b. His TV hasn't been working well.

2. a. She's been going to college.
    b. She's been working at a bank.

3. a. They've been waiting in a restaurant.
    b. They've been shopping in a supermarket.

4. a. Peter and Jane have been going to high school.
    b. Peter and Jane have been dating.

5. a. Their ceiling has been leaking.
    b. Their landlord has been complaining.

6. a. They've been writing all day.
    b. They've been riding their bicycles.

1. A. Something is the matter with my daughter Debbie.

   B. What seems to be the problem?

   A. She has a fever. And she's crying a lot.

   B. How long _____ has she been crying _____?

   A. _____ She's been crying _____ since yesterday afternoon.

   B. Can you bring her to see me at 2:00?

   A. Yes, I can. We'll be at your office at 2:00.

2. A. Mr. Burns? We're having some problems in our apartment.

   B. Oh? What's wrong?

   A. The ceiling is leaking. There's water all over the living room.

   B. How long _____?

   A. _____ since Monday morning.

   B. I'm glad you called me. I'll come over right away.

3. A. I'm afraid Michael is having some problems in school.

   B. Oh? What's the matter?

   A. He's been fighting with the other children.

   B. How long _____ with the other children?

   A. _____ with them for the past few weeks.

   B. That's very serious. I'll talk to him about it as soon as I get home.

   A. Thank you. I hope that helps.

(continued)

4. A. Hello, Charlie? This is Mrs. Graves. I'm afraid I've got some problems with my car.

B. What's wrong with it?

A. The engine is making a lot of noise.

B. How long _____ a lot of noise?

A. _____ a lot of noise since last week.

B. Can you bring it in on Wednesday morning?

A. Wednesday morning? That's fine. See you then.

5. A. We're having a terrible vacation!

B. That's a shame! What's happening?

A. It's raining. And it won't stop!

B. How long _____?

A. _____ since we arrived here three days ago.

B. That's too bad. I hope it stops raining soon.

A. So do I!

6. A. I'm having a problem with my neighbors.

B. That's too bad. What's the problem?

A. Their dogs bark all the time. They bark in the morning, they bark in the afternoon, and they bark all night.

B. How long _____?

A. _____ for several weeks.

B. Have you talked to your neighbors?

A. Yes. And they haven't done anything. I'm very frustrated.

bake	build	do	give	make	see	sell	take	write

1. I'm very tired. _____ *I've been giving* _____ piano lessons all day.

   _____ *I've given* _____ more than fifteen lessons since this morning.

2. I'm exhausted. _____ cakes since early

   this morning. _____ never _____ so many
   cakes in one day before.

3. We've been busy. _____ tee shirts at the mall

   all afternoon. _____ already _____ more than 75.

4. My children must be tired. _____ sandcastles

   on the beach all morning. Look! _____ already _____
   9 or 10!

5. I need a break. _____ inventory all day.

   _____ never _____ inventory for so many hours before.

6. Dr. Wilson looks very tired. _____ patients

   since 8 A.M. I think _____ more than 20.

7. You must be tired. _____ reports all day.

   _____ never _____ so many reports in one day before.

8. I'm exhausted! _____ smoothies all day.

   Believe it or not, I think _____ already _____ well over a
   hundred since we opened this morning.

9. Okay. You can stop. _____ sit-ups for more

   than an hour. _____ probably _____ more than a hundred.

N THEY'VE BEEN WORKING VERY HARD

The Sanchez family is having a big family reunion this weekend. Mr. and Mrs. Sanchez and their children have been working very hard to get ready for the big event.

| bake | hang up | look | make | plant | sing | throw out | vacuum | wash | write |

1. Mr. Sanchez ____has been washing____ windows. ___He's___ already _____washed_____ more than twenty windows.

2. _____ also _____ carpets. _____ already _____ all the carpets on the first floor of their house.

3. Mrs. Sanchez _____ decorations. _____ already _____ balloons in the living room and the dining room.

4. _____ also _____ casseroles. _____ already _____ five chicken casseroles and five tuna casseroles.

5. Their son, Daniel, _____ flowers and bushes. _____ already

   _____ yellow roses in their yard and two beautiful bushes near the front door.

6. _____ also _____ old newspapers. _____ already

   _____ all the old newspapers that were in their basement.

7. Their daughter, Gloria, _____. _____ already _____ ten apple pies and three dozen chocolate chip cookies.

8. _____ also _____ poems about each member of the family. _____

   already _____ a poem about her brother and a poem about her grandparents.

9. And while they've been working, the whole Sanchez family _____ songs.

   _____ already _____ more than fifty of their favorite songs.

10. Everybody in the Sanchez family is looking forward to the reunion. _____

    forward to it for several months. In fact, they have never _____ forward to anything as much as this weekend's family reunion.

THEY HAD DONE THAT BEFORE

1. Last night I was looking forward to having the piece of chocolate cake I *(put)* ___had put___ in the refrigerator. But when I opened the refrigerator, it was gone! Somebody

   (eat) _____ it!

2. Janet was very tired at work yesterday. She was exhausted because her husband

   (snore) _____ all night the night before and she hadn't slept.

3. Fred couldn't eat any lunch yesterday. He *(be)* _____ to the dentist that morning, and his mouth still hurt.

4. I didn't go out with Bill last Saturday night. I was upset because he *(go)* _____ out with my friend Denise the night before.

5. Jerry couldn't read his e-mail yesterday. He *(leave)* _____ his glasses at a concert the night before.

6. The man who delivered my computer couldn't assemble it because he *(assemble)* _____

   never _____ one before.

7. Jack didn't want to go to work yesterday. He was upset because he *(have)* _____ a terrible day at work the day before.

8. I fell asleep in Professor Baker's class yesterday. As soon as he started to speak, I realized

   that he *(give)* _____ the same lecture the week before.

9. We didn't watch *Jungle Adventure* on TV last night because we *(see)* _____ it twice at the movie theater.

10. Albert didn't buy anything at the mall last weekend because he *(spend)* _____ all his money at the mall the weekend before.

11. I didn't wear my pink-and-purple striped shirt to work yesterday. I wanted to, but then I

    remembered that I *(wear)* _____ it to work a few days before.

12. Frederick wanted to take a day off last week, but he decided that wasn't a very good idea

    because he *(take)* _____ two days off the week before.

13. My children didn't want spaghetti for dinner last night because I *(make)* _____ it for dinner three times the week before.

1. By the time I (get) ___got___ to the bank, it (close) ___had___ already
   ___closed___.

2. By the time I (do) _____ my monthly report, my supervisor
   (go) _____ already _____ home.

3. By the time we (arrive) _____ at the church, Jennifer and Jason
   (get) _____ already _____ married.

4. By the time we (drive) _____ to the ferry, it (sail) _____
   already _____ away.

5. By the time my friend (bring) _____ over his hammer, I
   (borrow) _____ already _____ one from my neighbor.

6. By the time the interviewer from the Blake Company
   (call) _____ me back, I (take) _____ already _____
   a job with the Drake Company.

7. By the time the doctor (see) _____ my mother, she
   (be) _____ in the emergency room for three hours.

8. By the time we (find) _____ our seats at the concert hall,
   the symphony (begin) _____ already _____.

9. By the time my taxi (drop) _____ me off at the train station,
   the train (leave) _____ already _____.

10. By the time I (stop) _____ speaking, I realized that at least
    half the audience (fall) _____ _____ asleep.

Q WHAT HAD THEY BEEN DOING?

1. I came down with the flu last week, and I had to cancel my camping trip. I was so

   disappointed. I *(plan)* _____had been planning_____ it for several months.

2. Tom and his girlfriend, Kathy, *(go out)* _____ for more than
   five years. When they broke up last week, everybody was very shocked.

3. Brian injured himself and wasn't able to participate in last week's swimming competition.

   He was extremely disappointed. He *(train)* _____ for it for months.

4. All our neighbors were surprised when the Carters sold their house last month and moved to

   a condominium in Arizona. They *(live)* _____ in our city all their lives.

5. The students in Mr. Frank's eighth-grade English class were upset when he suddenly decided

   to cancel the school play. They *(rehearse)* _____ for it all year.

6. I heard that Jonah got sick and couldn't take the SAT test. What's he going to do? He

   (prepare) _____ for the test since the beginning of the year.

7. I was disappointed that the jewelry store downtown went out of business last month.

   Everybody says the store *(have)* _____ a lot of financial problems.

8. We were all surprised when Brenda quit her job at the bank the other day. She

   (work) _____ there for more than fifteen years.

9. Nobody was surprised when Barry was fired from his job at the Langley Company. He

   (come) _____ to work late, and he *(fall)* _____
   asleep at his desk every afternoon.

10. It's a shame we arrived late for the space launch. We *(look)* _____
    forward to it all year.

11. My daughter Diane played the piano magnificently at her recital last night. I'm not

    surprised. She *(practice)* _____ for the recital for several
    months.

Listen. Then clap and practice.

I had been   planning   to call   Fernando.
By the time   I called,   he had moved   to Orlando.

I had been   hoping   to go out   with Ann.
By the time   I called,   she had left   for Japan.

I   had been thinking of   hiring   Bob.
By the time   I called,   he had found   a good job.

I   had been planning   to see friends   in L.A.
By the time   I got there,   they had moved   away.

S **LISTENING**

Listen to each word and then say it.

bother	both		busy	boss

1. <u>th</u>is
2. fa<u>th</u>er
3. <u>th</u>ey're
4. <u>th</u>at
5. wea<u>th</u>er

6. <u>th</u>ink
7. bir<u>th</u>day
8. <u>Th</u>eodore
9. <u>th</u>roat
10. Mar<u>th</u>a

11. mu<u>s</u>ic
12. doe<u>s</u>n't
13. day<u>s</u>
14. becau<u>s</u>e
15. love<u>s</u>

16. <u>s</u>ink
17. di<u>s</u>appointed
18. gue<u>ss</u>
19. <u>s</u>erious
20. look<u>s</u>

Fill in the missing letters and then read the conversation aloud.

s th

A. My bro _t_ _h_ er _T_ _h_ eodore doe__n't __ __ink he can go to __ __e __ __eater wi__ __ __ u__

   tomorrow becau__e he ha__ a __ore __ __roat.

B. Ano__ __er __ore __ __roat? __ __at's terrible! Didn't he ju__t get over one la__t

   __ __ursday?

A. __ __at's right. Believe it or not, __ __is is __ __e __ __ird __ore __ __roat he'__ had

   __ __is mon__ __. My poor bro__ __er alway__ get__ __ick when __ __e wea__ __er i__

   very cold.

B. I hope it i__n't __eriou__ __ __is time.

A. I don't __ __ink __o. __ __eodore __ays hi__ __ore __ __roat isn't bo__ __ering him too

   much, but bo__ __ my mo__ __er and fa__ __er __ay he'll have to re__t in bed for at lea__t

   a few day__. __ __ey're worried becau__e he i__n't eating any__ __ing, and __ __ey

   don't __ __ink he look__ very heal__ __y.

B. __ __en I gue__ __ he won't be going to __ __e __unday concert ei__ __er.

A. Probably not. And he'__ very di__appointed. He really love__ cla__ __ical mu__ic.

B. Well, I'm __orry our plan__ fell __ __rough. Plea__e tell __ __eodore I hope he feel__ better

   __oon. Oh, I almo__t forgot. My little si__ter Mar__ __a is having a __mall bir__ __day

   celebration today at __ __ree __ __irty. Would you like to come?

A. Ye__, of cour__e. __ __ank you very much.

WHAT SHOULD THEY HAVE DONE?

| buy | get | go | have | keep | see | sit | speak | study | take |

STUDENT BOOK
PAGES **15–30**

1. Angela was late this morning. She

   ___should have gotten___ to the train
   station earlier.

3. All the students failed Mrs. Baker's math

   exam. They _____
   harder.

5. Sally went to the beach yesterday, and it

   started to rain. She _____
   to the museum.

7. Nobody could hear you at the meeting.

   You _____ louder.

9. I'm sorry I threw away my ex-girlfriend's

   letters. I _____ them.

2. I'm really upset. I burned my cookies.

   I _____
   them out of the oven sooner.

4. I got sick because the chili was too spicy.

   I _____ the chicken.

6. We hated the science fiction movie in

   Cinema One. We _____
   the drama in Cinema Two.

8. I couldn't hear anything she said. I

   definitely _____ closer.

10. We're sorry we bought the small TV.

    We _____ the large one.

B GOOD ADVICE

1. I'm sorry. I can't read this.
   a. You shouldn't have written so legibly.
   b. You should have written more legibly. *(circled)*

2. I was stuck in traffic for two hours this morning.
   a. You should have driven to work.
   b. You shouldn't have driven to work.

3. Janet had a terrible stomachache last night.
   a. She shouldn't have eaten all the ice cream in her refrigerator.
   b. She should have eaten all the ice cream in her refrigerator.

4. Mr. Hopkins was uncomfortable at the beach.
   a. He shouldn't have worn a jacket and tie.
   b. He should have worn a jacket and tie.

5. We didn't like the movie on TV last night.
   a. You shouldn't have watched something else.
   b. You should have changed the channel.

6. Brian is confused in his Advanced Spanish class.
   a. He shouldn't have taken Beginning Spanish.
   b. He should have taken Beginning Spanish.

C YOU DECIDE: *Uncle Charlie's Advice*

| should have | shouldn't have |

All my life, my Uncle Charlie has always given me advice. He started giving me advice when I was a young boy.

1. Mom was angry because she tripped and fell when she came into my room this morning.

   Well, you should have _____,
   and you shouldn't have _____.

2. My parents were upset because I got a terrible grade on my last English test.

3. I wanted to go to the school dance with Amy, but by the time I asked her, she already had another date.

(continued)

Uncle Charlie was still giving me advice as I got older, got married, and had children.

4. Alice and I went to Hawaii after we got married, and it rained every day.

5. I'm really embarrassed. I ran in a marathon last weekend, and I finished last!

6. My son Ricky borrowed the car and had an accident. HE'S fine, but the car ISN'T!

Even now that I'm retired, Uncle Charlie STILL gives me advice.

7. I looked everywhere, but I couldn't find my glasses this morning!

8. I took my granddaughter to the opera last week, and she didn't like it!

9. I have a terrible backache. I played basketball with some of the kids in the neighborhood.

D WHAT MIGHT HAVE HAPPENED?

might have	may have

1. A. I wonder why Louise was late for work this morning.

   B. She (*might / miss*) ___might have missed___ the bus.

2. A. What happened to all the ice cream in the refrigerator?

   B. I'm not sure. The children (*may / eat*) ___may have eaten___ it.

3. A. I wonder why Donald isn't wearing his new watch.

   B. He (*may / break*) _____ it.

4. A. I called Aunt Gertrude all morning, and she wasn't home.

   B. She (*might / go*) _____ shopping.

5. A. Lucy didn't come to English class all last week.

   B. She (*may / be*) _____ sick.

6. A. I wonder why Nancy and Larry didn't come to my birthday party.

   B. They (*might / forget*) _____ about it.

7. A. It's 10 o'clock, and the Baxters haven't arrived at the party yet.

   B. Hmm. They (*might / lost*) _____ the directions.

E WHAT'S THE ANSWER?

1. My daughter is sick. She has a bad cold.
   (a.) She may have played with Timmy. He has a cold.
   b. She should have played with Timmy. He has a cold.

2. I wonder why Bertha didn't want to see the Eiffel Tower when she was in Paris.
   a. She should have seen it already.
   b. She might have seen it already.

3. James arrived late for the meeting.
   a. He should have called to tell us.
   b. He may have been late.

4. Rita decided to study Italian in college.
   a. She might have wanted to learn the language her grandparents speak.
   b. She shouldn't have wanted to learn the language her grandparents speak.

5. I wonder why we haven't seen our next-door neighbors recently.
   a. They should have gone on vacation.
   b. They might have gone on vacation.

6. We didn't like the food at that restaurant.
   a. We shouldn't have gone there.
   b. We may have gone there.

F. I DON'T UNDERSTAND IT!

could have

1. Grandma ___could have watched___ anything on TV last night. Why did she watch an old western she had already seen several times?

2. Tom went to his prom last night. He _____ any tuxedo he wanted to. Why did he wear a purple one?

3. I don't understand it. My daughter _____ anybody she wanted to. Why did she marry Herbert?

4. Your friends _____ their bicycles anywhere. Why did they ride them downtown during rush hour? It's very dangerous!

5. I don't understand it. My son _____ anything he wanted to. Why did he become a magician?

6. Those children _____ at the new skating rink in the center of town. Why did they skate on the town pond?

7. Barbara _____ any course she wanted to. I wonder why she's taking first-year French for the fourth time!

8. Richard Rockford _____ in any movie he wanted to. I wonder why he's in this awful movie!

9. You _____ anything you wanted to. Why did you make carrot soup with onions?

10. The Wilsons _____ their new son anything they wanted to. I wonder why they named him Mortimer!

11. Norman _____ his living room any color. I wonder why he painted it black!

12. Those tourists _____ at any restaurant in town. Why did they eat at MacDoodle's?

13. Frank and his wife _____ to a lot of interesting places for their vacation. Why did they go to Greenville?

14. I don't understand it. Sally _____ her composition about anything she wanted to. Why did she write about termites?

Listen. Then clap and practice.

He should have   studied   harder.

He could have   done   his best.

He should have   gotten   a good night's   sleep.

Then he might have   passed   the test.

She shouldn't have   packed   so much clothing.

She didn't need   all   that stuff.

She shouldn't have   taken   four bathing   suits.

One may have   been   enough.

I should have   taken   a shorter   break.

I shouldn't have come back   at three.

I missed   a meeting   at half past   two.

Now my boss   is mad   at me.

They shouldn't have   moved   to the suburbs.

They shouldn't have   bought   a car.

They should have   stayed   in the city,

Where everything's   close,   not far.

We should have   studied   Spanish

Before   we went   to Spain.

We could have   spoken   with the people   there

The minute   we left   the plane.

must have

1. A. Albert has been in a terrible mood all day.

   B. I know. He *(get up)* ___must have gotten up___ on the wrong side of the bed this morning.

2. A. Susie has a terrible stomachache.

   B. She *(eat)* _____ too many cookies for dessert.

3. A. I think I know you.

   B. I think I know you, too. We *(meet)* _____ before.

4. A. It's raining, and I can't find my umbrella.

   B. You *(leave)* _____ it at the office.

5. A. I didn't hear a word you said at the meeting.

   B. You didn't? I *(speak)* _____ too softly.

6. A. The boss gave everyone in our office a raise yesterday!

   B. He did? He *(be)* _____ in an excellent mood.

7. A. Ellen and her boyfriend, Bob, have stopped talking to each other.

   B. Really? They *(break up)* _____.

8. A. Beverly isn't driving an old car anymore.

   B. I know. She *(buy)* _____ a new one.

9. A. Johnny woke up crying in the middle of the night.

   B. I know. I heard him. He *(have)* _____ a bad dream.

10. A. The Gleasons' new living room sofa is beautiful.

    B. I know. It *(cost)* _____ a lot of money!

11. A. When I saw Donna this morning, she looked upset.

    B. Oh, no! She *(do)* _____ badly on her science test.

When Barbara and Edward Miller got home last Saturday afternoon, they found their front door was open and everything in the house was out of place. Someone must have broken into their house while they were out!

The first thing they saw was their attractive living room sofa. It was dirty and wet. Someone must have .... 1. Then they found their expensive new lamps on the floor. Someone must have .... 2. Their beautiful glass bowl from Italy wasn't in its usual place on the piano. Someone must have .... 3. Their computer was on, and there was a message on the screen. It said, " .... 4." Someone must have .... 5. They looked for their fax machine, but they couldn't find it. Someone must have .... 6.

Then they looked in the kitchen and found that the kitchen cabinets were all open. Someone must have .... 7. There was also an empty bottle of soda in the kitchen. Someone must have .... 8. And then they found that Barbara's car keys were missing! Someone must have .... 9. The door to the back porch was open, and the dog wasn't in the yard. Someone must have .... 10.

The Millers were very upset. They couldn't believe what had happened while they were out.

YOU DECIDE: *Might Have / Must Have*

1.

What did the Baxters name their new baby boy?

I'm not sure. They might have ...., or they might have ....

Didn't they want to name him after the president?

You're right. Then they must have ....

2.

Where did Elizabeth go on her vacation this year?

I'm not sure. She might have ...., or she might have ....

She sent me a picture of herself on a safari.

Oh. Then she must have ....

3.

What did Howard have for dinner at the restaurant last night?

I'm not sure. He might have ...., or he might have ....

Didn't you see tomato sauce all over his tie?

No, I didn't. Then he must have ....

4.

What vegetables did Martha plant in her garden this year?

I'm not sure. She might have ....
............................., or she might have ....
....

The last three times I went to her house, we had carrot juice, carrot cake, carrot cookies, and carrot pie!

Oh. Then she must have ....
....

5.

What did Mr. and Mrs. Williams do for their wedding anniversary?

I'm not sure. They might have ....
............................., or they might have ....
....

My brother saw them at the most expensive restaurant in town.

Oh. Then they must have ....
....

6.

Poor Angela! Her car wouldn't start this morning. How did she get to work?

I'm not sure. She might have ....
............................., or she might have ....
....

I think she asked her brother if his bicycle was working.

Oh. Then she must have ....
....

(continued)

7.

Why was your brother-in-law, Fred, fired?

I'm not sure. He might have ...., or he might have ....

Whenever I called him at work, he wasn't there.

Oh. Then he must have ....
....

K GRAMMARRAP: *What Must Have Happened?*

Listen. Then clap and practice.

Jonathan looks	happy.
He must have gotten	hired.
Mortimer looks	very sad.
He must have gotten	fired.

Timothy is	quite upset.
He must have failed	the test.
Jennifer is	smiling.
She must have done	her best.

Melanie looks	nervous.
She must have lost	her keys.
Her dog looks	very anxious, too.
He must have gotten	fleas.

Marvin came home	late last night.
He must have missed	the train.
His coat and hat and	shoes were wet.
He must have walked	in the rain.

L WHAT'S THE WORD?

could have	might have	should have
couldn't have	must have	shouldn't have

1. It's a very cold day. I _____ should have _____ worn a sweater. I'm sorry I didn't.

2. Mrs. Johnson never forgets her appointment with the dentist. But yesterday she forgot. I'm sure she _____ been very busy.

3. I _____ called you yesterday. I was in an important meeting all day.

4. Our English teacher was late for class today. He _____ overslept, or the bus_____ been late. I'm not sure.

5. Abigail is very absent-minded. Last week she got on the wrong train. She's very lucky. She _____ wound up in Canada!

6. I called your apartment all afternoon, and nobody answered. You _____ gone out.

7. I _____ gone skiing with you last Saturday. I had to take care of my niece.

8. My washing machine is broken. The repairperson said I never _____ tried to wash four pairs of sneakers and five pairs of jeans at the same time.

9. I wonder why my cousin Greg didn't want to come to the movie with us last night. He _____ seen it already. I'm not sure.

10. We _____ gone sailing on a windy day. We _____ gotten seasick!

11. You _____ swept your front porch. It looks so clean!

M LISTENING

Listen and choose the correct answer.

1. a. He must have gone to bed very late.
   b. He should have been very tired.

2. a. She must have called them later.
   b. She shouldn't have called them so late.

3. a. He should have missed the bus.
   b. He may have missed the bus.

4. a. You could have caught a cold.
   b. You should have done that.

5. a. He might have gotten a promotion.
   b. He must have been disappointed.

6. a. They should have rehearsed more.
   b. They must have remembered their lines.

7. a. She must have been home.
   b. She might have gone away.

8. a. He could have hurt himself!
   b. He shouldn't have hurt himself!

WHAT DOES IT MEAN?

Choose the correct answer.

1. Monica overslept.
   a. She came to work late.
   b. She stayed at a friend's house.
   c. She got up too early.

2. My doctor doesn't write legibly enough.
   a. He doesn't write enough.
   b. He doesn't write very often.
   c. I can't read anything he writes.

3. Vincent wound up in jail.
   a. He was dizzy.
   b. He asked a police officer to help him.
   c. He got arrested.

4. Eleanor was almost electrocuted.
   a. Now she's a senator.
   b. Now she's in the hospital.
   c. Now she's an electrician.

5. I owe you an apology.
   a. I'll pay you back.
   b. How much did it cost?
   c. I'm sorry I shouted at you.

6. They ate the entire pizza.
   a. They ate half the pizza.
   b. They ate all the pizza.
   c. They ate just a little pizza.

7. Martha is very understanding.
   a. She understands everything.
   b. She's very sympathetic.
   c. I understand everything she says.

8. He got up on the wrong side of the bed.
   a. Is he in a better mood now?
   b. Did he hurt himself?
   c. He didn't make his bed.

9. Their children refused to go.
   a. They didn't want to go.
   b. They wanted to go.
   c. They went there and returned.

10. We handed over the money.
    a. We held the money.
    b. They returned the money.
    c. We gave them the money.

11. They were having financial problems.
    a. They were having health problems.
    b. They were having family problems.
    c. They were having money problems.

12. Did your landlord evict you?
    a. Yes. We had to move.
    b. Yes. We envied them.
    c. Yes. We enjoyed the apartment.

13. Tony skipped work yesterday.
    a. He came to work early.
    b. He didn't come to work.
    c. He came to work late.

14. We ran up a very large bill.
    a. We spent a lot of money.
    b. We were very tired.
    c. We had never jogged so far.

15. Mrs. Grumble yelled at everybody today.
    a. She was ecstatic.
    b. She must have been in a good mood.
    c. She was very irritable.

16. He didn't act confidently at his interview.
    a. He didn't arrive on time.
    b. He didn't talk enough about his skills.
    c. I can't read anything he writes.

O **LISTENING**

Listen to each word and then say it.

1. f**i**ll—f**ee**l

2. f**i**lling—f**ee**ling

3. f**i**t—f**ee**d

4. h**i**s—he's

5. **i**t—**ea**t

6. kn**i**t—n**ee**d

7. l**i**ve—l**ea**ve

8. l**i**ving—l**ea**ving

9. r**i**ch—r**ea**ch

10. st**i**ll—st**ea**l

11. th**i**s—th**e**se

12. w**i**g—w**ee**k

13. w**i**ll—we'll

14. T**i**m—t**ea**m

15. h**i**t—h**ea**t

Listen and complete the sentences.

fill	feel

1. (a.) . . . today?
   b. . . . out this income tax form?

still	steal

2. a. . . . cars?
   b. . . . ride your bicycle to work?

this	these

3. a. . . . sneakers?
   b. . . . school?

knitted	needed

4. a. . . . a new sweater.
   b. . . . a new briefcase.

live	leave

5. a. . . . in a small house.
   b. . . . early every day.

living	leaving

6. a. . . . on the third floor.
   b. . . . on the next plane.

his	he's

7. a. . . . very tired.
   b. . . . alarm clock is broken.

It	Eat

8. a. . . . some potatoes instead.
   b. . . . wasn't very fresh.

this	these

9. a. . . . math problems.
   b. . . . homework assignment.

wig	week

10. a. . . . we're going to be busy.
    b. . . . needs a shampoo.

rich	reach

11. a. . . . New York?
    b. . . . and famous?

fill	feel

12. a. . . . it out right away.
    b. . . . a lot better soon.

fit	feed

13. a. . . . the animals very often.
    b. . . . me. They're too small.

It	Eat

14. a. . . . is my favorite recipe.
    b. . . . a little more.

still	steal

15. a. . . . go to high school.
    b. . . . cars anymore.

his	he's

16. a. . . . test was canceled.
    b. . . . getting married soon.

1. A. Did Picasso paint the *Mona Lisa*?

   B. No. The *Mona Lisa* __was painted__ by Leonardo da Vinci.

2. A. Did the Romans build the pyramids?

   B. No. The pyramids _____ by the Egyptians.

3. A. Did the chef serve you dinner at the Ritz?

   B. No. Dinner _____ by four waiters.

4. A. Did Bruce Springsteen compose "Yesterday"?

   B. No. "Yesterday" _____ by John Lennon and Paul McCartney.

5. A. Did Ponce de León discover America?

   B. No. America _____ by Christopher Columbus.

6. A. Did Charles Dickens write *Hamlet*?

   B. No. *Hamlet* _____ by William Shakespeare.

7. A. Did Queen Elizabeth wear this beautiful gown?

   B. No. This gown _____ by Jacqueline Kennedy.

8. A. This movie is incredible! Did Fellini direct it?

   B. No. It _____ by Steven Spielberg.

9. A. Did your parents take this prom picture of you and your girlfriend?

   B. No. This picture _____ by a photographer.

10. A. Did your mother bake this delicious cake?

   B. No. This cake _____ by my father.

YOU DECIDE: *At the Museum*

1. This car *(own)* _____ was owned _____

   by the president of ....

   It *(make)* _____

   by the ....

   Company in ....
   (year)

3. This beautiful necklace *(wear)* _____

   _____ by the famous actress

   ....

   It *(give)* _____ to her

   by .... It *(leave)*

   _____ to the museum
   by her children.

5. This letter *(write)* _____

   by ....

   to .... ,

   but it *(send)* _____ never _____ .

   It *(discover)* _____
   recently between the pages of an old
   book.

2. This airplane *(fly)* _____

   by ....

   in .... It *(design)* _____

   _____ by ....

   ....

4. These dinosaur skeletons *(find)* _____

   _____ by ....

   .... in Africa

   in .... Unfortunately, they
   (year)

   (forget) _____ by the
   museum for many years.

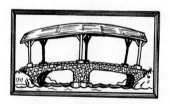

6. This impressive bridge *(build)* _____

   _____ in ....
   (city)
   more than 300 years ago. It *(begin)* _____

   _____ in 1520, and it *(finish)*

   _____ until 1600.

   (continued)

Activity Workbook **33**

7. This is one of ....'s

   earliest operas. It (compose) _____

   _____ in ....,
                                (year)

   and it (sung) _____

   for the first time in ....
                              (year)

8. This portrait ....

   ....

   ....

   ....

C GRAMMARRAP: *Who Took This Wonderful Photo of Jill?*

Listen. Then clap and practice.

A. Who took   this wonderful   photo of   Jill?

B. I think   it was taken   by her brother   Bill.

A. Who built that   beautiful   house   on the hill?

B. I think   it was built   by my cousin   Phil.

A. Who wrote   this interesting   book   about dance?

B. I think   it was written   by someone   in France.

A. Who drew   the plans for this   elegant   palace?

B. I think they were drawn   by a woman   from Dallas.

A. Who sang   that wonderful   Mexican   tune?

B. I think   it was sung   by a man   from Cancún.

A. Who did   this beautiful   picture   of snow?

B. I think   it was done   by Vincent   Van Gogh.

IT'S TOO LATE

Aunt Louise is a kind and generous person, but she's a little lazy. She wants to help her friends and family, but she never thinks about helping them until it's too late.

1. A. I'll be glad to help you do the dishes.

   B. Thank you, Aunt Louise, but _____ they've _____ already _____ been done _____.

2. A. Can I set the table for you?

   B. That's very nice of you, but _____ already _____.

3. A. Do you want me to iron the clothes today?

   B. Thanks, Aunt Louise, but _____ already _____.

4. A. I'll be glad to make Grandpa's doctor's appointment.

   B. That's very kind of you, but _____ already _____.

5. A. I think I'll take down the party decorations.

   B. Don't bother. _____ already _____.

6. A. Here. I'll sweep the floor.

   B. I appreciate it, but _____ already _____.

7. A. I'll be glad to buy flowers for the table.

   B. Thank you, Aunt Louise, but _____ already _____.

8. A. Do you want me to hang up the new portrait?

   B. I guess you haven't looked in the hall. _____ already _____.

LISTENING

Listen and decide what is being talked about.

1. a. the cookies
   b. the bed

2. a. the train
   b. the movie

3. a. the packages
   b. the letter

4. a. the scarf
   b. the fireplace

5. a. the presents
   b. the children

6. a. the bicycles
   b. the letters

7. a. the song
   b. the portrait

8. a. the books
   b. the cats

9. a. the meeting room
   b. the alarm

F NOTHING IS READY!

- [ ] make the beds
- [ ] sweep the porch
- [ ] prepare the salad
- [ ] feed the cat
- [ ] put the children to bed

A. What are we going to do? All our friends will be arriving soon, and nothing is ready. The

beds ___haven't been made___ [1]. The porch _____ [2]. The salad

_____ [3]. The cat _____ [4].

And the children _____ [5] to bed. I'm really upset.

B. Don't worry. Everything will be okay. We still have some time.

G AT THE HOSPITAL

- [x] take Mrs. Johnson's blood pressure
- [x] give Ms. Blake her injection
- [x] do Mr. Tanaka's cardiogram
- [x] tell Mrs. Wong about her operation
- [x] send Mr. Bacon home

A. How have all the patients been this morning? Have there been any problems?

B. Everything is fine, Doctor.

A. How is Mrs. Johnson this morning? ___Has___ [1] her blood pressure ___been taken___ [2] yet?

B. Yes, it has. And it wasn't as high as it was yesterday.

A. That's good. And _____ [3] Ms. Blake _____ [4] her injection?

B. Yes, she has. And we'll give her another at two o'clock.

A. What about Mr. Tanaka? _____ [5] his cardiogram _____ [6]?

B. Yes. It _____ [7] an hour ago.

A. Mrs. Wong looks upset. _____ [8] she _____ [9] about her operation?

B. Yes. I explained everything to her, and I think she understands.

A. And finally, is Mr. Bacon ready to leave the hospital?

B. He's MORE than ready! _____ [10] already _____ [11] home!

CAN WE LEAVE SOON?

	stop the mail
✔	turn off the lights
	set the alarm
	take out the garbage

A. Can we leave soon?

B. I think so. The mail ___has been stopped___ [1], and the lights _____

_____ [2].

A. Great!

B. Wait a minute! _____ [3] the house alarm _____ [4]?

A. No, it hasn't. But don't worry about it. I'll do it right away.

B. And now that I think of it, _____ [5] the garbage _____ [6]?

A. I'm not sure. Why don't I go and see?

I **CROSSWORD**

Across

2. The paychecks were _____ this morning.

4. Has the kitchen floor been _____ yet?

7. The Christmas presents were _____ in the attic last year.

Down

1. This picture was _____ by my daughter.

2. I hope your homework has already been _____.

3. This dress was _____ by Oleg Cassini.

5. The beds have already been _____.

6. That terrible speech was _____ by the president of our company.

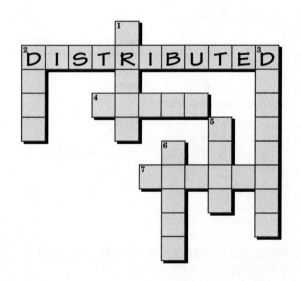

ERNEST HEMINGWAY

Read and then answer the questions below.

Ernest Hemingway is considered one of the most important modern American writers. He wrote six novels and more than fifty short stories. He also wrote many poems and newspaper articles.

Hemingway's books are lively and exciting. They are full of fighting, traveling, sports, love, and war. Hemingway's life was also lively and exciting.

When he was a young high school student, Hemingway played football, boxed, and wrote for the school newspaper. He ran away from home when he was fifteen years old, but he returned and finished high school in 1917. He never went to college.

Hemingway wanted to fight in World War I, but he was rejected by the army. Instead, he went to war as an ambulance driver and was badly injured.

In 1921, Hemingway went to Paris and started writing seriously. He stayed there for six years. His first novel, *The Sun Also Rises*, was written when he was still in Paris. It made him very famous.

In 1937, Hemingway went to Spain as a journalist to write about the Spanish Civil War. In 1944 he returned to Europe and wrote newspaper articles about World War II. Although he wasn't in the army, it is believed he did more fighting than writing during the war.

What's the Answer?

1. Why is Hemingway considered an important writer?
   a. He wrote many interesting works.
   b. He liked sports.
   c. He lived in many different countries.

2. What *didn't* Ernest Hemingway write about?
   a. Fighting.
   b. Traveling.
   c. Cooking.

3. What did Hemingway do when he was fifteen years old?
   a. He ran a long way.
   b. He left home.
   c. He went to high school.

4. Which of these statements about Hemingway is true?
   a. He finished high school.
   b. He went to college.
   c. He didn't play any sports in high school.

5. Why didn't Hemingway serve in the army?
   a. He wanted to fight.
   b. The army didn't want him.
   c. He didn't want to fight.

6. Which of these statements about Hemingway *isn't* true?
   a. He was a journalist for a while.
   b. He wrote about the Spanish Civil War.
   c. *The Sun Also Rises* was written in Spain.

Mr. and Mrs. Wilson (rob) _____were_____ 1 _____robbed_____ 2 last month. Their TV, their

computer, and all of their beautiful living room furniture (steal) _____ 3

_____ 4. In fact, nothing (leave) _____ 5 _____ 6 in the living room

except the rug. Fortunately, Mrs. Wilson's gold necklace (take) _____ 7 _____ 8.

She was glad because it had been (give) _____ 9 to her by her husband many years ago.

The thief (see) _____ 10 _____ 11 driving away from the house in a small

black van. The neighbors called the police, and the man (arrest) _____ 12

_____ 13. He (send) _____ 14 _____ 15 to jail for seven years.

A day after the robbery, the living room furniture, the computer, and the TV

(return) _____ 16 _____ 17. The sofa had (rip) _____ 18

_____ 19, but fortunately everything else was okay.

 L   LISTENING

Listen and choose the correct answer.

1. a. Yes. It's already been fixed.
   b. No. It hasn't been swept yet.

2. a. Yes. It's already been set.
   b. Yes. It's already been set up.

3. a. It was written by my uncle.
   b. It was taken by my wife.

4. a. I'm sorry. They've already been sung.
   b. I'm sorry. They've already been hung.

5. a. He was hurt in an accident.
   b. He was offered a better job.

6. a. She's already been lent.
   b. She's already been sent.

7. a. Yes. It's been rejected.
   b. Yes. It's been approved.

8. a. She was hired by the Blaine Company.
   b. She was fired by the Blaine Company.

9. a. They've already been hung.
   b. They've already been sung.

10. a. Yes. It's already been baked.
    b. Yes. It's already been set.

11. a. It's already been read.
    b. It's already been played.

12. a. She's been taken to the hospital.
    b. She's been invited to a wedding.

M YOU DECIDE: *A Famous Composer*

.... ¹ is an extremely talented composer. She has written many beautiful sonatas. Her compositions *(perform)* _____ have ² _____ been ³ _____ performed ⁴ in Asia, in the United States, and in

.... ⁵. Her symphonies are often *(hear)* _____ ⁶ on the radio.

Ms. .... ⁷ started to compose music when she was .... ⁸ years old. She *(give)* _____ ⁹ _____ ¹⁰ a composition book for her birthday, and she knew right away that she wanted to be a composer.

In 1985, she sent some of her sonatas and a symphony to the .... ¹¹ Symphony Orchestra, but all these early compositions *(reject)* _____ ¹² _____ ¹³. Ms. .... ¹⁴ was disappointed, but she continued to compose. Finally, in 1994, several of her sonatas *(recorded)* _____ ¹⁵ _____ ¹⁶ by the

.... ¹⁷ Symphony Orchestra.

It took many years before Ms. .... ¹⁸'s music *(appreciate)* _____ ¹⁹

_____ ²⁰. At first, her music *(consider)* _____ ²¹ _____ ²² strange because it was new and different, and it *(understand)* _____ ²³ not easily

_____ ²⁴. Most people couldn't hear the beautiful melodies. Today, of course, Ms.

.... ²⁵ is highly *(respect)* _____ ²⁶ by composers all over the world.

In 1996, she wrote her most famous symphony called "...................................... ²⁷." A year later, it *(used)* _____ ²⁸ _____ ²⁹ as the music in a very successful movie. Since then, she has written three other symphonies that *(play)* _____ ³⁰ _____ ³¹

_____ ³² all over the world.

In 2001, Ms. .... ³³ *(hurt)* _____ ³⁴ _____ ³⁵ badly in a car accident. She composed a sonata about this terrible accident. In 2002, Ms.

.... ³⁶ *(choose)* _____ ³⁷ _____ ³⁸ best composer of the year. She *(invite)* _____ ³⁹ _____ ⁴⁰ to play her music at the White House in Washington, D.C.

N WHAT ARE THEY SAYING?

bake	promote	rewrite	take in
clip	repair	set up	wash

1. A. The president is concerned. Is his speech ready?

   B. It'll be ready soon. _____It's_____

   _____being rewritten_____ .

2. A. Why are you taking the bus to work?

   B. My car was in an accident. _____

   still _____ .

3. A. Is this Bob's Bakery? I'm calling about the cake I ordered.

   B. I'm sorry. It isn't ready yet. _____

   still _____ .

4. A. Should I pick up my pants at the tailor's?

   B. Not yet. _____ still

   _____ .

5. A. Is Carla going to quit her job at the Internet company?

   B. No. She's decided to stay because

   _____ next week.

6. A. Is the meeting room ready?

   B. Not yet. _____ still _____

   _____ .

7. A. What happened to the shirt I wore to the baseball game yesterday?

   B. _____ .
   It was very dirty.

8. A. Hello. This is Mrs. Vickers. When is my poodle going to be ready?

   B. Very soon. His hair _____

   _____ right now.

O GrammarRap: *Spring Cleaning*

Listen. Then clap and practice.

The family's   getting organized.

The beds   are being made.

The kitchen's   being swept and cleaned.

The bills   are being paid.

The sheets and towels   are being washed

And dried   and put away.

The rugs   are being vacuumed.

Spring cleaning starts   today.

Good morning, and welcome to your tour of Bob and Betty's Ice Cream Factory. We make the best ice cream in the world, and you're going to see how we do it! You'll learn a lot about how ice cream *(made)* _____ is _____[1] _____ made _____[2] at Bob and Betty's! Let's begin.

In this room, cream *(take)* _____[3] _____[4] out of our large refrigerators. Then the cream *(put)* _____[5] _____[6] into this machine. The cream *(mix)* _____[7] _____[8] for about forty minutes in this machine. While the cream is mixing, sugar *(pour)* _____[9] _____[10] slowly into the cream by our ice cream makers.

In the next room, the flavors *(prepare)* _____[11] _____[12]. Today we are making banana nut ice cream. Right now, different kinds of nuts *(chop)* _____[13] _____[14] _____[15] in a large chopper. It's a very expensive machine, but it chops the nuts very quickly. Also, bananas *(slice)* _____[16] _____[17] _____[18] in our new computer-controlled slicing machine.

When the nuts and bananas are ready, they *(add)* _____[19] _____[20] to the sugar and cream in a special machine that *(invent)* _____[21] _____[22] by Betty a few years ago.

The ice cream *(keep)* _____[23] _____[24] in a large cold room until it *(sent)* _____[25] _____[26] by trucks all over the country.

That is the end of our tour. Thank you for visiting our factory, and we invite you to go to our tasting room, where our delicious ice cream can *(enjoy)* _____[27] _____[28] by all our visitors.

WHAT DOES IT MEAN?

Choose the correct answer.

1. I've got to take in my suit.
   a. It's too big.
   b. It's too small.
   c. It's too hot.

2. You're required to go to the meeting.
   a. You might go to the meeting.
   b. You don't have to go to the meeting.
   c. You have to go to the meeting.

3. Lois ran up a big phone bill.
   a. She talked on the telephone a lot.
   b. She didn't use her cell phone.
   c. The phone company gave her a phone.

4. Ms. Johnson was promoted.
   a. She was hired.
   b. She was given a more important job.
   c. She was fired.

5. Parking is permitted here.
   a. You can't park here.
   b. You can park here.
   c. You have to park here.

6. Tom is distributing the mail right now.
   a. He's giving it to everyone.
   b. He's sending it to everyone.
   c. He's opening the mail for everyone.

7. I was rejected by Harvard University.
   a. I'll work there next year.
   b. I'll be a student there next year.
   c. I'll attend another college next year.

8. You'll be allowed to vote when you're older.
   a. You'll be required to vote.
   b. You'll be permitted to vote.
   c. You'll want to vote.

9. She was offered the position.
   a. She was given the job.
   b. She was told about the position.
   c. She was taken off the position.

10. Where are the decorations?
    a. They've already been offered.
    b. They've already been set.
    c. They've already been hung up.

11. This is a beautiful portrait.
    a. Who directed it?
    b. Who invented it?
    c. Who painted it?

12. I'm going overseas to work.
    a. My boss is going to watch me.
    b. I'm going to work in another country.
    c. I'm going to work near the water.

13. I'm confident about the future.
    a. I'm concerned about the future.
    b. I'm confused about the future.
    c. I'm positive about the future.

14. My son was chosen "Student of the Month."
    a. He must be afraid.
    b. He must be thrilled.
    c. He must be hung up.

R **LISTENING**

Listen and choose the correct answer.

1. a. When will it be finished?
   b. When was it finished?

2. a. When will it be ready?
   b. How long ago did you finish?

3. a. They've been made.
   b. They're being made.

4. a. I didn't receive mine.
   b. Someone is distributing them.

5. a. It's being set up.
   b. It's been set up.

6. a. I see. When will it be ready?
   b. Good. I'll come over right away.

7. a. When will they be ready?
   b. How long have they been ready?

8. a. I don't want to disturb them.
   b. How long ago did you feed them?

A. Complete the sentences.

Ex. My son can swim very well. ___He's___ ___swum___ for many years.

1. Can you speak Chinese? I can speak it very well. _____ _____ it for many years.

2. Can you ride horses? My daughter _____ _____ horses for a long time.

3. When did you take your break? I _____ _____ my break yet.

4. When are you going to eat lunch? I'm hungry. I _____ _____ lunch yet.

5. When are you going to write your composition? I _____ _____ mine yet.

     Bob _____ his composition a little while ago.

6. How long _____ you and your husband _____ married?

7. My daughter _____ _____ studying English for the past few hours.

8. Paul didn't see a movie last weekend. He _____ _____ a movie the weekend before.

9. By the time I got to the plane, it _____ already _____ off.

10. I'm sorry to hear that Debbie and her boyfriend broke up. They _____ _____

     _____ out for several years.

B. Complete the sentences.

could have	might have	must have	should have	shouldn't have

(give) *Ex.* You ___shouldn't___ ___have___ ___given___ Howard eggs for breakfast. He's allergic to them.

(practice) 1. Boris has won every chess game he's played today. He _____ _____

     _____ a lot.

(do) 2. I don't have anything to wear today. I _____ _____ _____ my laundry.

(leave) 3. Timmy can't find his homework. He _____ _____ _____ it at home,

     or he _____ _____ _____ it on the bus. He can't remember.

(build) 4. The Ace Corporation _____ _____ _____ their office building anywhere. It was a mistake to build it here.

(study)   **5.** You did very well on your test. You _____ _____ _____ a lot.

(wear)   **6.** It's hot in here. I _____ _____ _____ a heavy sweater to work today.

(feed)   **7.** You _____ _____ _____ Rex. He's been hungry all morning.

(fall)   **8.** Terry shouldn't have stood on that broken chair. She _____ _____
_____ .

(spend)   **9.** I _____ _____ _____ ten dollars, or I _____ _____ _____
twelve dollars. I can't remember.

C. Complete the sentences.

(write)   **Ex.** This poem ___was___ ___written___ in 2001.

(draw)   **1.** This picture _____ _____ by a famous artist.

(repair)   **2.** I can't drive my car to work. _____ still _____ _____ .

(give)   **3.** My wife _____ _____ _____ a raise twice this year.

(teach)   **4.** Every student should _____ _____ a foreign language.

(do)   **5.** Nobody has to do the dishes. _____ already _____ _____ .

(take in)   **6.** Your pants aren't ready yet. _____ still _____ _____ .

(choose)   **7.** Margaret _____ _____ "Employee of the Year."

(make)   **8.** This is a very interesting novel. I think it should _____ _____ into
a movie.

(send)   **9.** Grandma is still in the hospital. She _____ _____ _____
home yet.

D. Listening

Listen and choose the correct answer.

Ex. (a.) When was it completed?
    b. When will it be completed?

4. a. When was it completed?
    b. When will it be done?

1. a. When will you finish taking them?
    b. When did you finish taking them?

5. a. Good. I'll pick it up soon.
    b. When will it be ready?

2. a. How much longer will it take?
    b. How long ago did you hang them up?

3. a. They're being made.
    b. They've been made.

A INVENTIONS THAT CHANGED THE WORLD

Read the article on student book page 47 and answer the questions.

1. Alexander Fleming discovered _____.
   a. bacteria
   b. X-rays
   c. an antibiotic
   d. mold

2. The first screws were _____.
   a. mass-produced
   b. made of wood
   c. used to hold things together
   d. small

3. The first Nobel Prize in Physics was for _____.
   a. the screw
   b. the telephone
   c. the television
   d. the X-ray machine

4. Alexander Graham Bell was NOT _____.
   a. deaf
   b. a teacher
   c. a doctor
   d. an inventor

5. The first telephone call was made _____.
   a. in 1895
   b. to Thomas Watson
   c. to Alexander Graham Bell
   d. by Thomas Watson

6. Computers were very large before the invention of _____.
   a. the telephone
   b. the X-ray machine
   c. the television
   d. the microchip

7. The first _____ was built for the army.
   a. computer
   b. telephone
   c. television
   d. X-ray machine

8. The first television was made of _____.
   a. paper and glass
   b. needles and a bicycle
   c. common household objects
   d. wires and tubes

STUDENT BOOK
PAGES 47–50

B FACT FILE

Look at the Fact File on student book page 47 and answer the questions.

1. The Fact File presents information in the form of _____.
   a. a graph
   b. a major invention
   c. a time line
   d. an article

2. The Fact File helps the reader understand the article about inventions because _____.
   a. it gives the information in a visual form
   b. it summarizes the article
   c. it gives opinions about inventions
   d. it tells about the lives of inventors

3. The microscope was invented _____ years after the printing press.
   a. 50
   b. 100
   c. 140
   d. 150

4. _____ in the twentieth century.
   a. CDs were NOT invented
   b. X-rays were NOT discovered
   c. Penicillin was NOT discovered
   d. Gas-powered cars were NOT invented

Read the information on student book page 48 and answer the questions.

1. This information is presented in the form of _____.
   a. an article
   b. photographs with captions
   c. a chart
   d. a timeline

2. _____ was built in the 12th century.
   a. The Taj Mahal
   b. The Great Wall of China
   c. The Temple of Angkor Wat
   d. Machu Picchu

3. _____ was a city.
   a. Stonehenge
   b. The Taj Mahal
   c. The Colosseum
   d. Tenochtitlan

4. _____ is older than the Colosseum.
   a. Machu Picchu
   b. Stonehenge
   c. The Taj Mahal
   d. The Temple of Angkor Wat

5. _____ is a modern wonder of the world.
   a. Machu Picchu
   b. The Great Wall of China
   c. The Temple of Angkor Wat
   d. The Panama Canal

6. The Taj Mahal and the Pyramids were both built _____.
   a. in Egypt
   b. more than 1000 years ago
   c. for the dead
   d. with machines

7. 200,000 to 300,000 people _____.
   a. built Tenochtitlan
   b. lived in Tenochtitlan
   c. live in Mexico City
   d. built the Taj Mahal

8. No one knows _____.
   a. why Shah Jahan built the Taj Mahal
   b. why the Egyptians built the Pyramids
   c. who built Stonehenge
   d. why the Temple of Angkor Wat was built

9. _____ was definitely NOT a place of worship.
   a. The Colosseum
   b. Stonehenge
   c. The Temple of Angkor Wat
   d. Machu Picchu

10. People say that the Great Wall is visible from the moon because it is _____.
    a. in the mountains
    b. very tall
    c. very bright
    d. very long

11. Machu Picchu was *abandoned* in the 1500s means _____.
    a. everybody left
    b. construction was finished
    c. it was destroyed
    d. it was dedicated

12. Which sentence best *summarizes* this information?
    a. These places were constructed for religious purposes.
    b. The world is full of modern and ancient wonders.
    c. The United Nations helps preserve these wonders.
    d. These are the most popular places to visit in the world.

D AROUND THE WORLD: Writing

What is another wonder of the world that you know about? Write a paragraph about it. Use some of these words in your paragraph: *begun, built, completed, constructed, dedicated, designed, established, inhabited, preserved, rebuilt, repaired, used.*

INTERVIEW

Read the interview on student book page 49 and answer the questions.

1. Sam Turner has been a photojournalist _____.
   a. since he was ten
   b. since he won a competition
   c. for ten years
   d. for twenty years

2. He grew up in Australia because _____.
   a. his parents were American
   b. his parents were Australian
   c. his parents worked there
   d. he loved the Outback

3. Many people encouraged him to study photography because _____.
   a. he took many family trips
   b. they were impressed by his photos
   c. he was given a camera
   d. he went to photography school

4. His photography is inspired by _____.
   a. his parents
   b. his camera
   c. the national photo competition
   d. nature

5. His most important life event was _____.
   a. winning a photo contest
   b. hiking to the top of Mt. Everest
   c. climbing to the base of Mt. Everest
   d. returning to Mt. Everest

6. You can infer that he would NOT be inspired to take photographs of _____.
   a. the Statue of Liberty
   b. the Grand Canyon
   c. the Mississippi River
   d. Yellowstone National Park

F **YOU'RE THE INTERVIEWER!**

Interview a classmate, a neighbor, or a friend. Use the chart below to record the person's answers. Then share what you learned with the class.

What is something you are very interested in? How did you become interested in that?	
What has been the most memorable event in your life so far?	
What do you dream about doing someday?	

G **FUN WITH IDIOMS**

Choose the best response.

1. I was blown away by the cost of the dinner.
   a. I know. It was very windy.
   b. I was surprised, too.
   c. I didn't enjoy it either.
   d. I also thought it was delicious.

2. My bus was held up by the parade.
   a. My bus was stuck in traffic, too.
   b. Yes. I saw your bus in the parade.
   c. I'm glad you arrived early.
   d. I agree. It was a colorful parade.

3. Since you didn't call me, I was left in the dark about our plans.
   a. Yes. It was dark when I called.
   b. I'm sorry the lights went out.
   c. I'm sorry you didn't know.
   d. I'm sorry it was dark.

4. Tom was given the ax last week.
   a. That's wonderful news!
   b. I'm sure he's very happy.
   c. That's a very unusual gift.
   d. What a shame!

WE'VE GOT MAIL!

Choose the words that best complete each sentence.

1. The wheel _____ in 3500 B.C.
   a. is invented
   b. invented
   c. was invented
   d. has invented

2. The Taj Mahal _____ in the 17th century.
   a. was built
   b. has built
   c. built
   d. was building

3. All students _____ to take the final exam.
   a. be required
   b. are required
   c. requiring
   d. have required

4. The instructions _____ on the board.
   a. were writing
   b. written
   c. wrote
   d. were written

5. The stop sign _____ by a truck last night.
   a. is hit
   b. hit
   c. was hit
   d. was being hit

6. Children should not _____ to see that movie.
   a. allow
   b. allowed
   c. are allowed
   d. be allowed

Choose the sentence that is correct and complete.

7. a. The oil in my car was changing.
   b. The oil in my car be changed.
   c. The oil in my car being changed.
   d. The oil in my car was changed.

8. a. He be taken to the hospital.
   b. He took to the hospital.
   c. He was taken to the hospital.
   d. He was took to the hospital.

9. a. The new curtains were hung.
   b. The new curtains be hung.
   c. The new curtains been hung.
   d. The new curtains being hung.

10. a. The house built in 1953.
    b. The house was built in 1953.
    c. The house has built in 1953.
    d. The house being built in 1953.

11. a. She been told about the meeting.
    b. She not be told about the meeting.
    c. She being told about the meeting.
    d. She wasn't told about the meeting.

12. a. The winner be chosen soon.
    b. The winner chose soon.
    c. The winner will be chosen soon.
    d. The winner was chose soon.

"CAN-DO" REVIEW

Match the "can do" statement and the correct sentence.

____ 1. I can tell about my work experience.

____ 2. I can ask about the duration of an activity.

____ 3. I can tell about the duration of an activity.

____ 4. I can evaluate my own activities.

____ 5. I can make a deduction.

____ 6. I can apologize.

____ 7. I can express agreement.

____ 8. I can express uncertainty.

____ 9. I can offer to do something.

____ 10. I can react to good news.

a. I've been waiting for the plumber all morning.

b. Tony must have missed the bus.

c. Do you want me to do the dishes?

d. I'm sorry.

e. I've flown airplanes for many years.

f. I'm not sure.

g. That's wonderful!

h. How long have you been studying for the test?

i. I think so, too.

j. I shouldn't have eaten that entire dessert.

THEY DIDN'T SAY

A. Were you just talking to George and Janet on the phone?

B. Yes. They called from California.

A. How are they?

B. They're fine.

A. The last time I heard from them, they were building a new house. Where are they living now?

B. I don't know _____*where they're living now*_____ [1]. They didn't say.

A. Where is Janet working?

B. I have no idea _____ [2]. She didn't say.

A. How are their children?

B. I'm not sure _____ [3]. They didn't say.

A. Tell me about George. When will he be starting his new job?

B. I don't know _____ [4]. He didn't say.

A. I really miss George and Janet. When are they going to come to New York?

B. I'm not sure _____ [5]. They didn't say.

A. When will their new house be finished?

B. I don't know _____ [6]. They didn't say.

A. What have they been doing since we saw them last summer?

B. I have no idea _____ [7]. They didn't say.

A. Why haven't they e-mailed us?

B. I'm not sure _____ [8]. They didn't say.

A. This is ridiculous! I'm going to call them tonight. What's their telephone number?

B. I'm sorry. I don't know _____ [9]. They didn't say.

I'M NOT THE PERSON TO ASK

1. A. What does this painting mean?

    B. I have no idea _____ *what this painting means* _____.

2. A. Why does Robert always get to school so early?

    B. I don't know _____.

3. A. When did the ice cream truck come by?

    B. I have no idea _____.

4. A. Where does Margaret work?

    B. I don't remember _____.

5. A. How did Sam break his arm?

    B. I don't know _____.

6. A. Why did Alice rewrite her novel?

    B. I have no idea _____.

7. A. What time does the concert begin?

    B. I'm not sure _____.

8. A. When does the bank open tomorrow?

    B. I have no idea _____.

9. A. What did we do in French class yesterday?

    B. I can't remember _____.

10. A. Where did Mom and Dad go?

    B. I have no idea _____.

11. A. How much does a quart of milk cost?

    B. I don't know _____.

C. TOO MANY QUESTIONS!

A. Daddy, when did you learn to drive?

B. I can't remember _____ when I learned to drive _____¹.
It was a long time ago.

A. Why doesn't Grandma drive?

B. I don't know _____².
You'll have to ask her.

A. Daddy, I've been thinking . . . Why is the sky blue?

B. I don't know _____³.

A. How do birds learn to fly?

B. I'm not sure _____⁴.

A. Why are clouds white?

B. I don't know _____⁵.

A. What time does the zoo open tomorrow?

B. I'm sorry. I don't know _____⁶.

A. Daddy, do you remember the mouse that was in our attic last winter?

B. Yes, I do.

A. Where is that mouse now?

B. I don't know _____⁷.

A. Daddy, why _____⁸?

B. I have no idea _____⁹.

A. Daddy, when _____¹⁰?

B. I don't remember _____¹¹.

A. When will we be home?

B. I hope we'll be home soon.

WHAT ARE THEY SAYING?

1. Do you know _____?
   a. what time it is
   b. what time is it

2. Could you possibly tell me _____?
   a. when will the train arrive
   b. when the train will arrive

3. Can you tell me _____?
   a. where do they live
   b. where they live

4. I'm not sure _____.
   a. how long they're going to stay
   b. how long are they going to stay

5. I'm sorry. I have no idea _____.
   a. when will she be back
   b. when she'll be back

6. Could you possibly tell me _____?
   a. how I can get there from here
   b. how can I get there from here

7. I can't remember _____.
   a. why does she want to talk to me
   b. why she wants to talk to me

8. Do you have any idea _____?
   a. whose glasses are these
   b. whose glasses these are

9. Could you please tell me _____?
   a. how much this costs
   b. how much does this cost

10. I don't remember _____.
    a. what are our plans for the weekend
    b. what our plans are for the weekend

E **LISTENING**

Listen and decide what is being talked about.

1. a. a bus
   b. a movie

2. a. a word
   b. a person

3. a. a cake
   b. a photograph

4. a. a bicycle
   b. a car

5. a. a movie
   b. a train

6. a. a plane ticket
   b. a TV

7. a. the packages
   b. the restrooms

8. a. the books
   b. the animals

F **GRAMMARRAP:** *Do You Know How Long This Flight Will Take?*

Listen. Then clap and practice.

A. Do you know   how long   this flight   will take?

   Do you know   what kind of   food   they'll make?

   Do you know   what movie   they'll show   on the plane?

   Do you know   what time   we'll get   to Spain?

B. I don't know   how long   this flight   will take.

   I'm not sure   what kind of   food   they'll make.

   I don't know   what movie   they'll show   on the plane.

   I have no   idea when we'll get   to Spain.

YOU DECIDE: *What Are They Saying?*

Answer the questions with any vocabulary you wish.

1.

> How much does this bicycle cost?

A. Can you tell me _____ how much _____

_____ this bicycle costs _____?

B. ....

....

2.

> Where is the nearest clinic?

A. Could you possibly tell me _____

_____?

B. ....

....

3.

> Whose cell phone is this?

A. Do you have any idea _____

_____?

B. ....

....

4.

> Why have you been late to work all week?

A. Could you tell me _____

_____?

B. ....

....

5.

> When will my dog be ready?

A. Can you tell me _____

_____?

B. ....

....

6.

How long have we been driving?

A. Do you have any idea _____

_____?

B. ....

....

7.

Why is Johnny sitting in a puddle?

A. Can you tell me _____

_____?

B. ....

....

8.

When does the post office open?

A. Do you by any chance know _____

_____?

B. ....

....

9.

What's in the "Chicken Surprise Casserole"?

A. Could you please tell me _____

_____?

B. ....

....

10.

When will you be getting out of here?

A. Do you know _____

_____?

B. ....

....

Listen. Then clap and practice.

A.   What   did he do?

B.   I don't know   what he did.

A.   Why   did he hide?

B.   I don't know   why he hid.

A.   Where   did he go?

B.   I don't know   where he went.

A.   What   did he spend?

B.   I don't know   what he spent.

A.   What   did she say?

B.   I don't know   what she said.

A.   What   did she read?

B.   I don't know   what she read.

A.   Where   was her purse?

B.   I don't know   where it was.

A.   What   does she do?

B.   I don't know   what she does.

A.   What   did they buy?

B.   I don't know   what they bought.

A.   What   did they bring?

B.   I don't know   what they brought.

A.   What   did they sell?

B.   I don't know   what they sold.

A.   Who   did they tell?

B.   I'm not sure   who they told.

1. Do you know _____?
    (a.) whether parking is permitted here
    b. if is parking permitted here

2. Can you tell me _____?
    a. if will the library be open tomorrow
    b. if the library will be open tomorrow

3. Do you by any chance know _____?
    a. whether it's going to rain this weekend
    b. if is it going to rain this weekend

4. Could you please tell me _____?
    a. whether does this bus stop at the mall
    b. if this bus stops at the mall

5. Do you have any idea _____?
    a. if they were upset
    b. whether were they upset

6. Can you possibly tell me _____?
    a. if the bus will be arriving soon
    b. if will the bus be arriving soon

7. Do you know _____?
    a. whether they're coming to our party
    b. if are they coming to our party

8. Can you tell me _____?
    a. whether did I pass the test
    b. if I passed the test

9. Does our superintendent know _____?
    a. if the plumber is coming soon
    b. whether is the plumber coming soon

10. Do you by any chance know _____?
    a. whether I'm going to be fired
    b. if am I going to be fired

J LISTENING

Listen and decide where these people are.

1. (a.) a beach
    b. a parking lot

2. a. a department store
    b. a laundromat

3. a. a playground
    b. a theater

4. a. a parking garage
    b. a parking lot

5. a. a train station
    b. a gas station

6. a. a classroom
    b. a restaurant

7. a. a bakery
    b. a lake

8. a. a post office
    b. a supermarket

9. a. a zoo
    b. a bank

K GRAMMARRAP: *Gossip*

Listen. Then clap and practice.

A. Do you know   whether David   is dating   Diane?

    Do you know   if Irene   is married   to Stan?

    Can you tell me   if Bob   is in love   with Elaine?

    Do you know   if they really   met   on a plane?

B. I don't know   whether David   is dating   Diane.

    I'm not sure   if Irene   is married   to Stan.

    I can't tell you   if Bob   is in love   with Elaine.

    And I really   don't know   if they met   on a plane.

L RENTING AN APARTMENT

> Questions to Ask the Rental Agent
>
> 1. Has it been rented yet?
> 2. Is there an elevator in the building?
> 3. Does the kitchen have a microwave?
> 4. Are pets allowed?
> 5. Is there a bus stop nearby?
> 6. Does the landlord live in the building?
> 7. Does the apartment have an Internet connection?
> 8. _____
> 9. Can I see the apartment today?

A. Hello. This is Mildred Williams. I'm calling about the apartment at 119 Appleton Street. Can you tell me _____ *if it's been rented yet* _____ [1]?

B. Not yet. But several people have called. Would you like to see it?

A. Yes, but first I have a few questions. According to the newspaper, the apartment is on the fifth floor. Can you tell me _____ [2]?

B. Yes. As a matter of fact, there are two elevators.

A. I see. And do you know _____ [3]?

B. It has a dishwasher, but it doesn't have a microwave.

A. Also, do you by any chance know _____ [4]?

B. I don't know. I'll check with the landlord.

A. Can you tell me _____ [5]?

B. Yes. The downtown bus stops in the front of the building.

A. That's very convenient. Can you also tell me _____ [6]?

B. Yes, he does. And all the tenants say he takes very good care of the apartments.

A. Do you know _____ [7]?

B. Yes, it does. It's a very modern building.

A. And could you please tell me _____ [8]?

B. I'm not sure. I'll have to find out and let you know.

A. You've been very helpful. Do you know _____ [9]?

B. Certainly. Stop by our office at noon, and I'll take you to see it.

Ask the Admissions Office

1. How many students go to your school?
2. Do I have to take any special examinations?
3. How do I get an application form?
4. Are the classes difficult?
5. Are the dormitories noisy?
6. What kind of food do you serve in the cafeteria?
7. What do students do on weekends?
8. How much does your school cost?
9. ....
10. ....

Hello. My name is Robert Johnson, and I'm interested in studying at your college. I'd like to ask you a few questions.

Certainly. My name is Ms. Lopez. I'll be happy to answer your questions.

1. Can you tell me _____*how many*_____ _____*students go to*_____ _____*your school*_____?

2. Do you know _____ _____ _____?

3. Can you tell me _____ _____ _____?

(continued)

4. Also, could you tell me _____ _____ _____ _____ ?

5. I've heard the dormitories are large.

Do you know _____ _____ ?

6. Do you by any chance know _____ _____ _____ ?

7. Can you tell me _____ _____ _____ ?

8. I'm a little worried about expenses.

Can you tell me _____ _____ ?

9. Can you also tell me _____ _____ ?

10. And do you know _____ _____ ?

1. My doctor says that if I exercise every day, _____ healthier.
    a. I'm
    (b.) I'll be

2. If Alan _____ stuck in traffic today, he'll be late for work.
    a. gets
    b. will get

3. If _____ the lottery tomorrow, I'll have a lot of money.
    a. I'll win
    b. I win

4. If we get to the theater early, _____ to get good seats.
    a. we're able
    b. we'll be able

5. If you decide to apply for a promotion, _____ probably get it.
    a. you'll
    b. you

6. If they _____ to pay the rent next week, their landlord will call them.
    a. forget
    b. will forget

7. If Amanda oversleeps this morning, _____ the bus.
    a. she misses
    b. she'll miss

8. If you _____ for Jack Strickland, you'll have an honest president.
    a. will vote
    b. vote

9. If the weather is warm, _____ to the beach tomorrow.
    a. I'll go
    b. I go

10. If _____ Melanie, I'm sure I'll be happy for the rest of my life.
    a. I'll marry
    b. I marry

B SCRAMBLED SENTENCES

1. late   she'll   lot   tonight.   to   at   If   do,   has   work   Barbara   the   a   office

    _____ *If Barbara has a lot to do* _____ , _____ *she'll work late at the office tonight.* _____

2. attic   energetic,   he'll   his   If   this   clean   Tom   weekend.   feels

    _____ , _____

3. cake   about   decide   have   to   If   diet,   I'll   I   dessert.   forget   for   my

    _____ , _____

4. income   weather   tomorrow,   the   home   nice   If   I'll   forms.   stay   isn't   my   tax   fill   out   and

    _____ , _____

5. clinic   see   I   If   I'll   cold   Dr. Lopez.   still   a   go   tomorrow,   have   the   to   and

    _____ , _____

Activity Workbook   **57**

YOU DECIDE: *If*

1. If I'm in a good mood, ...

2. .... if I'm in a bad mood.

3. If .... ,
   he'll speak more confidently.

4. .... , you'll be disappointed.

5. If I can afford it, ...

6. .... , we'll be very surprised.

7. If I'm invited to the White House, ...

8. You'll get lost if ....

9. You'll regret it if ....

10. .... , you won't regret it.

D **LISTENING** 🔊

Listen and complete the sentences.

1. a. . . . I go to a movie.
   (b.) . . . I'll go to a concert.

2. a. . . . I'm on a diet.
   b. . . . I'll stay on a diet.

3. a. . . . we miss the train.
   b. . . . we'll miss the train.

4. a. . . . they rent a DVD.
   b. . . . they'll go dancing.

5. a. . . . we're late for school.
   b. . . . we'll have to walk to work.

6. a. . . . you miss the test.
   b. . . . you'll miss the exam.

7. a. . . . the teacher is boring.
   b. . . . the teacher will be bored.

8. a. . . . it isn't too expensive.
   b. . . . it won't cost as much.

9. a. . . . he complains to his boss.
   b. . . . he'll quit his job.

10. a. . . . you'll decide to visit me.
    b. . . . you want to go jogging.

11. a. . . . she has time.
    b. . . . she won't be too busy.

12. a. . . . I take them to the doctor.
    b. . . . I'll call the nurse.

13. a. . . . we have too much work.
    b. . . . we'll be too busy.

14. a. . . . she doesn't study.
    b. . . . she won't work harder.

Listen. Then clap and practice.

If it rains, I'll take a taxi.

If it snows, I'll take the train.

If it's sunny, I'll ride my brand new bike,

The one that was made in Spain.

If it's hot, they'll wear their sandals.

If it's cold, they'll wear their boots.

If the weather is nice, they'll go to the beach.

And swim in their bathing suits.

If the party starts at seven o'clock,

We'll plan to arrive at eight.

If we're tired, we'll come home early.

If we aren't, we'll get home late.

If I'm hungry, I'll have a midnight snack.

If I'm sleepy, I'll go to bed.

If I'm wide awake, I'll stay up late

With a book I haven't read.

1. Remember, if you plan to have your wedding outside, it _____.
   (a.) might rain
   b. rains

2. If we take the children to visit their grandparents, they _____ sore throats.
   a. might give
   b. might give them

3. If Marvin breaks up with Susan, he _____ trouble finding another girlfriend.
   a. might have
   b. might be

4. If you go to bed too late, _____ have trouble getting up on time for work.
   a. you might
   b. you'll might

5. If you don't take that job, you _____ it for the rest of your life.
   a. regret
   b. might regret

6. If you have trouble seeing well, _____ rejected by the army.
   a. I might be
   b. you might be

7. If our teacher tries to break up that fight, _____.
   a. he might get hurt
   b. he might hurt

8. If we take the children to see the skeletons at the museum, they _____.
   a. might scare
   b. might be scared

G YOU DECIDE: *What Might Happen?*

| if _____ might _____ |

1. A. I still have a cold, and I feel terrible.

   B. That's too bad. Why don't you drink tea with honey?

   If _____you drink_____ tea with honey, ...you might......

   ....feel better soon......................... .

2. A. Should I put more pepper in the casserole?

   B. I'm not sure. If _____ more pepper in

   the casserole, ...

   ....

3. A. It's the boss's birthday tomorrow. Why don't we send her flowers?

B. I'm not sure. If _____

her flowers, ...

....

4. A. I'm thinking of skipping English class today,

B. I don't think you should. If _____

English class, ...

....

5. A. Mrs. Wong, I really enjoy taking violin lessons with you. I'm going to practice every day.

B. I'm happy to hear that. If _____

every day, ...

....

6. A. Good-bye!

B. Please don't stay away too long! If _____

away for a long time, ...

....

7. A. Danny, I don't think you should go hiking in the woods by yourself.

B. Why not?

A. If _____ by yourself, ...

....

8. A. You've known each other for only a few weeks. I don't think you should get married so soon.

B. Why not?

A. If _____ so soon, ...

....

if _____ might _____

1. A.   I don't think I'll ever learn to speak English well.

    B.   Why don't you ....?

    If _____,

    _____ you might learn _____ to speak English better.

2. A.   I feel exhausted.

    B.   Why don't you ....?

    If _____,

    _____ more energetic.

3. A.   I can't fall asleep.

    B.   Maybe you should ....

    If _____,

    _____ more easily.

4. A.   I've been feeling depressed lately.

    B.   I think you should ....

    If _____,

    _____ a lot better.

5. A.   My girlfriend and I had a terrible argument. She won't go out with me anymore.

    B.   Why don't you ....?

    If _____,

    _____ with you again.

1. I like to play tennis every day.

I hope it _____ tomorrow.
  a. rains
  b. doesn't rain

2. My daughter sometimes rides her bicycle too fast.

I hope she _____ hurt.
  a. gets
  b. doesn't get

3. I'm going to a party this Saturday night.

I hope you _____ a good time.
  a. have
  b. don't have

4. My daughter's wedding is next week.

I hope the weather _____ bad.
  a. is
  b. isn't

5. I love my new flowerpot.

I hope it _____ and break.
  a. falls off
  b. doesn't fall off

6. I'm going to refuse to marry Jonathan.

I hope you _____ it later.
  a. don't regret
  b. regret

7. My poodle loves to splash in puddles.

I hope she _____ dirty.
  a. gets
  b. doesn't get

J LISTENING

Listen and choose the polite response.

1. a. I hope so.
   b. I hope not.

2. a. I hope so.
   b. I hope not.

3. a. I hope so.
   b. I hope not.

4. a. I hope so.
   b. I hope not.

5. a. I hope so.
   b. I hope not.

6. a. I hope so.
   b. I hope not.

7. a. I hope so.
   b. I hope not.

8. a. I hope so.
   b. I hope not.

9. a. I hope so.
   b. I hope not.

10. a. I hope so.
    b. I hope not.

11. a. I hope so.
    b. I hope not.

12. a. I hope so.
    b. I hope not.

1. A. Do you think it will rain tomorrow?

   B. I hope not. If _____it rains_____ tomorrow, we'll have to cancel our picnic.

   And if ___we have to cancel___ the picnic, everybody will be disappointed.

   A. You're right. I hope ___it doesn't rain___ tomorrow.

2. A. Do you think it'll be cold tonight?

   B. I hope not. If _____ tonight, our car won't start in the morning.

   And if our car _____ in the morning, we'll have to walk to work.

   A. You're right. I hope _____ tonight.

3. A. Do you think it'll be a hot summer?

   B. I hope not. If _____ a hot summer, the office will be very warm.

   And if the office _____ very warm, it'll be impossible to work.

   A. You're right. I hope _____ a hot summer.

4. A. Do you think our TV will be at the repair shop for a long time?

   B. I hope not. If our TV _____ at the repair shop for a long time, we won't have anything to do in the evening.

   And if _____ anything to do in the evening, we'll go crazy.

   A. You're right. I hope _____ at the repair shop for a long time.

1. A. I've gotten up early every day this semester, and I haven't missed anything important.

   B. That's great! I hope get up early again tomorrow.

      It's the last class and the last exam.

   A. I know. ⬚ definitely get up early tomorrow.

2. A. Do you think tomorrow's exam will be difficult?

   B. I hope not. If ⬚ difficult, I'll probably do poorly.

      And if poorly, my parents disappointed.

3. A. What happened? You overslept and missed the exam!

   B. I have a terrible cold. I'm going to call my professor now.

      I hope she ⬚ angry. If she ⬚ angry, ⬚ give me a bad grade.

4. A. What did your professor say?

   B. She said she hopes ⬚ feel better soon. If ⬚ feel better tomorrow, ⬚ take the exam at 2 o'clock.

      If ⬚ still sick tomorrow, ⬚ take the exam on Wednesday morning.

1. If my apartment _____ bigger, I would be more comfortable.
   a. was
   b. were ⟨circled⟩

2. If you _____ more, you'd be stronger.
   a. exercised
   b. exercise

3. If it were a nice day today, _____ to the park.
   a. we'll go
   b. we'd go

4. If I _____ more, I'd be happy working here.
   a. got paid
   b. get paid

5. If I were going to be here this weekend, _____ a movie with you.
   a. I'll see
   b. I'd see

6. If _____ more friends in our apartment building, we'd be much happier living there.
   a. we had
   b. we have

7. If you _____ up your engine more often, you'd get better gas mileage.
   a. tune
   b. tuned

8. If _____ more, you'd feel more energetic.
   a. you sleep
   b. you slept

9. If she were more careful, _____ a better driver.
   a. she'd be
   b. she'll

10. If you _____ older, we'd let you stay up later.
    a. were
    b. are

11. If Rick and Rita had more in common, I'm sure _____ get along better with each other.
    a. they'd
    b. they

12. If the president _____ more concerned about the environment, he'd do something about it.
    a. is
    b. were

N LISTENING

Listen and choose the correct answer based on what you hear.

1. a. George probably feels energetic.
   b. George probably feels tired. ⟨circled⟩

2. a. The musicians aren't very talented.
   b. The musicians are talented.

3. a. He's very aggressive.
   b. He isn't aggressive enough.

4. a. Bob's car needs to be tuned up.
   b. Bob's car doesn't need to be tuned up.

5. a. They have a lot in common.
   b. They don't have a lot in common.

6. a. She cares a lot about her students.
   b. She isn't a very good teacher.

7. a. Their school needs more computers.
   b. Their school has enough computers.

8. a. The cookies aren't sweet enough.
   b. The cookies are sweet enough.

O YOU DECIDE WHY

1. **A.** Mr. Montero, why doesn't my daughter Lisa get better grades in English?

B. She doesn't _____*do her homework carefully*_____ ,

she doesn't _____ ,

she doesn't _____ ,

and she doesn't _____ .

If she _____*did her homework carefully*_____ ,

if she _____ ,

if she _____ ,

and if she _____ ,

_____ much better

grades. She's a very intelligent girl.

2. **A.** What's wrong with me, Dr. Green? Why don't I feel energetic anymore? I'm only thirty years old, and I feel exhausted all the time.

B. You don't _____ ,

you don't _____ ,

you don't _____ ,

and you _____ .

If you _____ ,

if you _____ ,

if you _____ ,

and if you _____ less,

_____ much more energetic.

3. A. How do you like your new car?

B. It's better than my old one, but I really don't like it very much.

A. That's too bad. Why not?

B. It doesn't _____,

it doesn't _____,

I'm not _____,

and my husband _____.

If _____,

if _____,

if _____,

and if _____,

_____ my car a
lot more. I guess all cars have their problems.

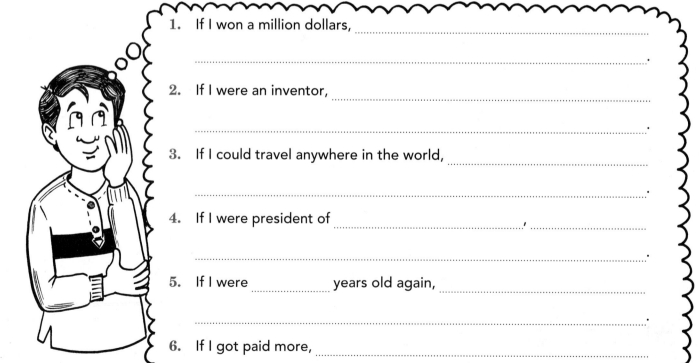

P **YOU DECIDE:** *What Would You Do If . . . ?*

1. If I won a million dollars, _____
_____.

2. If I were an inventor, _____
_____.

3. If I could travel anywhere in the world, _____
_____.

4. If I were president of _____,
_____.

5. If I were _____ years old again, _____
_____.

6. If I got paid more, _____
_____.

_d_ 1. If this party weren't so boring,

_____ 2. If I didn't hate working here,

_____ 3. If I didn't have a big exam tomorrow,

_____ 4. If I weren't such a careless driver,

_____ 5. If I weren't a vegetarian,

_____ 6. If I weren't always late,

_____ 7. If I weren't allergic to cats,

_____ 8. If they weren't in love,

_____ 9. If I didn't like the outdoors so much,

_____ 10. If your car weren't so old,

_____ 11. If we didn't make so much noise,

a. I wouldn't have so many accidents.

b. I wouldn't be sneezing so much.

c. you wouldn't have so many problems with it.

d. we wouldn't want to leave so early.

e. people wouldn't have to wait for me.

f. I wouldn't go hiking every weekend.

g. I wouldn't be so nervous.

h. I wouldn't always order vegetables.

i. the neighbors wouldn't be complaining.

j. I wouldn't be looking for another job.

k. they wouldn't hold hands all the time.

R YOU DECIDE: *What Are They Saying?*

1. I haven't had anything to eat all day.   You must _____be very hungry_____.

2. My son didn't get accepted into the college he wanted.   That's too bad. He must _____ _____.

3. You've been driving for the past six hours. You must _____.

(continued)

4. Ted went out with Jean on Monday, with Jane on Tuesday, with Joan on Wednesday, and with Jen on Thursday.

He must ....
....

5. My neighbors spend every weekend at the beach. Last weekend they went water-skiing, and this weekend they're going sailing.

They must really ....
....

6. My daughter got the highest grade in her class.

She must .... ,
and you must ....

7. I'm going to miss something important in school tomorrow.

Really? You must ....
....

8. Last weekend I made three pies and four cakes. This weekend I'm going to make cookies.

No kidding! You must ....
....

9. My son is going to be the star of his school play this weekend.

He must .... ,
and you must ....

10. My husband has been watching a football game on TV all day, and there's a big game he's going to watch tonight.

He must really .... ,
and you must ....

11. You've been complaining about this movie since it started. You

must ....
....

1. Rita works overtime every night. She must want to get a raise.

   If _____ *she didn't want to get* _____ a raise,

   she _____ *wouldn't work overtime* _____ every night.

2. Jimmy is hiding under the bed. He must be afraid of the dark.

   If _____ of the dark,

   he _____ under the bed.

3. Stephanie runs ten miles every day. She must want to win the marathon this weekend.

   If _____ the marathon,

   she _____ ten miles every day.

4. My friend Gary wears a green shirt every day. He must love the color green.

   If _____ the color green,

   he _____ a green shirt every day.

5. My sister Karen makes a lot of mistakes on her homework. She's very careless.

   If _____ ,

   she _____ a lot of mistakes on her homework.

6. Gregory goes to the health club every day. He must want to lose weight.

   If _____ weight,

   he _____ to the health club every day.

(continued)

7. Andy is all dressed up. He must have a big date tonight.

If _____ a big date tonight,

he _____ all dressed up.

8. I'm driving very slowly because there's a police car behind me.

If _____ a police car behind me.

I _____ so slowly.

T **YOU DECIDE:** *Why Don't Mr. and Mrs. Miller Like Their Neighborhood?*

Mr. and Mrs. Miller don't like their neighborhood because ....,

....,

....,

....,

and ....

If _____,

if _____,

if _____,

and if _____,

_____ their neighborhood a lot more.

GRAMMARRAP: *If I Lived Near the Sea*

Listen. Then clap and practice.

If I lived   near the sea,   I'd swim   every day.

If I had   a guitar,   I'd learn   how to play.

If I were younger   and stronger,   I'd lift   heavy weights.

If I weren't   so shy,   I'd go out   on more dates.

If Tom could speak   Spanish,   he'd travel   to Spain.

If Ann had   a raincoat,   she'd walk   in the rain.

If Jack were   an actor,   he'd star   in a play.

If we weren't   so busy,   we'd go sailing   today.

GRAMMARRAP: *If I Didn't Like Desserts*

Listen. Then clap and practice.

If I didn't like   desserts,   I wouldn't eat   cake.

If I didn't like   meat,   I wouldn't eat   steak.

If I weren't   so happy,   I wouldn't   be smiling.

If I weren't working   late,   I wouldn't be   filing.

If she didn't like   pets,   she wouldn't have   a cat.

If he didn't play   baseball,   he wouldn't have   a bat.

If they weren't   so clumsy,   they wouldn't always   fall.

If you weren't   my friend,   I wouldn't always   call.

W LISTENING

Listen to each word and then say it.

1. <u>m</u>ight
2. <u>m</u>aybe
3. <u>m</u>ushroo<u>m</u>
4. su<u>mm</u>er
5. i<u>m</u>prove
6. re<u>m</u>e<u>m</u>ber
7. poe<u>m</u>s
8. war<u>m</u>
9. fa<u>m</u>ous

10. <u>n</u>ight
11. <u>n</u>ever
12. <u>n</u>oo<u>n</u>
13. su<u>nn</u>y
14. Su<u>n</u>day
15. i<u>n</u>crease
16. explai<u>n</u>
17. telepho<u>n</u>e
18. fa<u>n</u>tastic

X NORMAN'S BROKEN KEYBOARD

**Norman's keyboard is broken. The m's and the n's don't always work.
Fill in the missing m's and n's and then read Norman's letters aloud.**

1.

Dear A <u>m</u> y,

   I really e <u>n</u> joyed visiti__g you i__ your __ew apart__e__t.
It's o__e of the __icest apart__e__ts I've ever see__. I liked
everythi__g about it: the __oder__ kitche__ a__d bathroo__,
the elega__t livi__g roo__ and di__i__g roo__, a__d the
su____y bedroo__s. I ca__'t believe there's eve__ a garde__
with le__o__ and ora__ge trees i__ fro__t of the buildi__g.
I thi__k you'll be very happy i__ your __ew __eighborhood.
It's certai__ly very co__ve__ie__t to be so __ear a
super__arket, a __ovie theater, a__d a trai__ statio__.
   I'__ looki__g forward to seei__g you agai__ a__d
__eeti__g your __ew __eighbors.

                              Si__cerely,

                              __or__an

2.

To Who__ It __ay Co__cer__:

I a__ writi__g to reco__ __e__d __ax __iller for the job of co__puter progra__ __er at the ABC Co__puter Co__pa__y. Duri__g the __i__e years I've k__ow__ hi__, he's bee__ a__ excelle__t e__ployee a__d a ki__d a__d ho__est frie__d. He's __ever __issed a day's work at our co__pa__y, a__d he's always bee__ o__ ti__e. But __ost i__porta__t, __ax __iller really u__dersta__ds what __akes a good co__puter progra__ __er.

Si__cerely,

__or__a__ Brow__

__a__ager

XYZ Co__puter Co__pa__y

3.

Dear Bria__,

I just fi__ished readi__g your __ost rece__t poe__s, a__d i__ __y opi__io__, they're a__azi__g. The poe__ about the e__viro__ __e__t is very origi__al, but __y favorite o__es are "__issi__g __y __other" a__d "U__der __y U__brella."

Accordi__g to __y wife a__d frie__ds, you're beco__i__g fa__ous i__ __a__y foreig__ cou__tries, a__d your poe__s are bei__g tra__slated i__to Russia__, Chi__ese, Ger__a__, Spa__ish, a__d Japa__ese. I thi__k that's fa__tastic!

Have you begu__ writi__g your __ew __ovel yet? I wo__der whe__ we'll be heari__g more about it.

__or__a__

4.

Dear __ichael,

Re__e__ber whe__ you explai__ed to __e how to __ake your __other's fa__ous chicke__ a__d __ushroo__ casserole? Well, I __ade so__e for di__ __er last __ight, a__d I'__ afraid so__ethi__g __ust have go__e wro__g. I__ight have bur__t the chicke__, or __aybe I did__'t put i__ e__ough o__io__s a__d __ushroo__s. I do__'t k__ow what happe__ed, but I k__ow I __ust have __ade so__e __istakes because __obody e__joyed it very __uch. To__ and __a__cy did__'t co__plai__, but they said yours was __uch __ore delicious.

Do you thi__k you could se__d your __other's recipe to __e by e-__ail so I ca__ try it again? Whe__ you explai__ed it to __e, I should have writte__ it dow__.

__or__a__

A. Fill in the blanks.

Ex. *(What time does the plane arrive?)*

Could you please tell me _____ <u>what time the plane arrives</u> _____?

1. *(When will the next train be leaving?)*

   Can you tell me _____?

2. *(Was Michael at work yesterday?)*

   Do you know _____?

3. *(How much does this suit cost?)*

   Can you please tell me _____?

4. *(Is there a laundromat nearby?)*

   Could you tell me _____?

5. *(Why did David get up so early?)*

   Do you know _____?

6. *(Did Martha take her medicine this morning?)*

   Do you know _____?

7. *(How long have we been waiting?)*

   Do you have any idea _____?

B. Complete the sentences.

Ex. If we can afford it, _____<u>we'll take</u>_____ a vacation next summer.

1. I'll send you an e-mail if I _____ the time.

2. If Uncle Fred were more careful, _____ a better driver.

3. If Mrs. Bell didn't enjoy classical music, _____ to concerts every weekend.

4. If I _____ a raise soon, I'll complain to my supervisor.

5. If you stay up too late tonight, _____ get a good night's sleep.

6. We're having a picnic this Sunday. I hope _____ rain.

7. Tomorrow is the most important game of the year. I hope our team _____.

8. My parents _____ extremely disappointed if I fail tomorrow's French test.

9. If you _____ your dog more often, he wouldn't be so hungry.

C. Complete the sentences.

Ex. Albert doesn't have many friends because he isn't outgoing enough.

If he ___were___ more outgoing, ___he'd have___ a lot of friends.

1. Caroline feels tired all the time because she works too hard.

   If she _____ so hard, _____ so tired all the time.

2. David doesn't get good grades in school because he doesn't study enough.

   If he _____ more, _____ better grades.

3. Allison and Paul don't get along with each other because they don't have enough in common.

   If they _____ more in common, _____ better with each other.

4. Nellie is very careless. She makes a lot of mistakes when she types.

   If she _____ so careless, _____ a lot of mistakes.

D. Listening

Listen and complete the sentences.

Ex. (a.) . . . I'll play tennis.
   b. . . . I'd play tennis.

1. a. . . . I'd be late for work.
   b. . . . I'll be late for work.

2. a. . . . I wouldn't make so many mistakes.
   b. . . . I won't make so many mistakes.

3. a. . . . you didn't study for the test.
   b. . . . you don't study for the test.

4. a. . . . I'd see a movie.
   b. . . . I'll see a movie.

5. a. . . . she'll go out with you.
   b. . . . she'd go out with you.

A THE MUSIC OF WISHES AND HOPES

Read the article on student book page 79 and answer the questions.

1. Which song was made popular by a singing group?
   a. "If I Were a Rich Man"
   b. "If I Were a Bell"
   c. "If I Had a Hammer"
   d. "If I Could Change the World"

2. _____ of the songs described in the article were first performed in musicals.
   a. Two
   b. Three
   c. Four
   d. None

3. In _____ of the songs, the wish is for wealth.
   a. one
   b. two
   c. three
   d. four

4. Lee Ann Womack is a _____.
   a. folk singer
   b. rock singer
   c. Broadway singer
   d. country music singer

5. You can infer that a Grammy Award is given for _____.
   a. songs
   b. books
   c. acting
   d. writing a poem

6. In "If I Had a Million Dollars," the word *exotic* means _____.
   a. expensive
   b. beautiful
   c. unusual
   d. very large

7. In all of these songs, the common wish of the singers is to have _____.
   a. love
   b. peace
   c. time
   d. happiness

8. From this article, you can infer that the music of wishes and hopes is _____.
   a. always about relationships
   b. found in many different types of music
   c. the most popular music theme
   d. loved by everyone

B MUSIC LYRICS AND METAPHORS

A *metaphor* is a figure of speech. It describes two different things or people as being the same in some way. Answer these questions about metaphors in the article.

1. In the song from the musical *Guys and Dolls*, a happy Sarah describes herself as _____.
   a. a gambler at a gate
   b. the man she loves
   c. a swinging bell
   d. a ringing bell

2. In the song from the movie *Phenomenon*, the singer's metaphor is that he and the girl he loves _____.
   a. would go to the center of the universe
   b. would get married
   c. would be a king and queen
   d. would change the world

3. In another song in the article, saving money in a bank is compared to _____.
   a. saving money to buy a house
   b. winning a Grammy Award
   c. saving time in a bottle
   d. being rich

4. Another famous song in the article describes using a hammer as a metaphor for _____.
   a. building a house for a family
   b. working for peace
   c. ringing a bell
   d. singing a song

C FACT FILE

Look at the Fact File on student book page 79 and answer the questions.

1. The word _____ is the most popular of the three words in song titles.
   a. "hope"
   b. "wish"
   c. "if"

2. The word _____ is not in any of the song titles in the article.
   a. "hope"
   b. "wish"
   c. "if"

D AROUND THE WORLD

Read the article on student book page 80 and answer the questions.

1. You make a wish if you catch something in _____.
   a. Jamaica
   b. Japan
   c. Korea
   d. Ireland

2. If you hear coins splash into water three times in _____, your wishes will come true.
   a. the United States
   b. Asia
   c. South America
   d. Europe

3. Make a wish when you blow out candles on a cake _____
   a. in the evening
   b. at midnight
   c. on your birthday
   d. when you look at the moon

4. Coins are used for making wishes in _____ of the traditions described in the article.
   a. two
   b. three
   c. four
   d. five

5. _____ of the traditions described in the article involve looking at the sky.
   a. One
   b. Two
   c. Three
   d. Four

6. People in the United States are likely to make a wish with a wishbone on _____.
   a. Valentine's Day
   b. July 4th
   c. Thanksgiving
   d. New Year's Day

7. "Star light, star bright, first star I see tonight" is a _____.
   a. wish
   b. tradition
   c. custom
   d. poem

8. In the New Year's Eve tradition with grapes, the *chimes* of the clock refer to _____.
   a. the sounds of the clock
   b. the hands of the clock
   c. grapes
   d. midnight

9. If you throw a *pebble* into a well to make a wish, you throw _____.
   a. a leaf
   b. a nut
   c. a small stone
   d. a candle

10. The tradition for making wishes with _____ requires two people.
    a. a wishbone or a coin
    b. a nut or a leaf
    c. candles or grapes
    d. a wishbone or a nut

Read the interviews on student book page 81 and answer the questions.

1. The man on the left wouldn't want to quit his job because _____.
   a. he has too much free time
   b. he loves his job
   c. he works very hard
   d. he wouldn't know how to use his time

2. _____ of the people would stop working.
   a. One
   b. Two
   c. Three
   d. Four

3. _____ of the people would help family members.
   a. One
   b. Two
   c. Three
   d. Four

4. _____ of the people would save the money.
   a. One
   b. Two
   c. Three
   d. Four

5. You can infer that *debts* are _____.
   a. money you owe
   b. banks
   c. people
   d. jobs

6. One man would give money to charities. You can infer that _____.
   a. he's retired
   b. he already has a lot of money
   c. he's generous
   d. he works

Interview a classmate, a neighbor, or a friend. Use the chart below to record the person's answers. Then share what you learned with the class.

What would you do if you won a million dollars?	
Would you keep working or going to school? Why or why not?	
Would you give money to people? Who would you give it to?	
Would you give any money to charities? Which ones?	

Match the question and the correct answer.

____ 1. What would you say to someone who always makes you feel happy?

____ 2. What would you say if someone hurt your feelings very badly?

____ 3. What would you say to someone you would do anything for?

____ 4. What would you say to a friend who often ignores you?

a. You're breaking my heart.

b. You light up my life.

c. You're a heel!

d. You've got me wrapped around your little finger.

Choose the words that best complete each sentence.

1. We hope they _____ on time for dinner.
   a. will   c. will be
   b. are   d. be

2. He hopes he _____ a raise.
   a. is going to get   c. is getting
   b. will get   d. gets

3. They hope it _____ tomorrow.
   a. is raining   c. doesn't rain
   b. will rain   d. won't rain

4. She hopes the bus _____ late.
   a. isn't   c. is going to be
   b. won't be   d. will be

5. I hope I _____ for the team.
   a. will be chosen   c. will choose
   b. am chosen   d. am choosing

6. We hope we _____ the train.
   a. won't miss   c. don't miss
   b. are missing   d. aren't going to miss

Choose the sentence that is correct.

7. a. If I was tired, I wouldn't go with you.
   b. If I weren't tired, I would go with you.
   c. If I weren't tired, I will go with you.
   d. If I wasn't tired, I would go with you.

8. a. If she wasn't busy, she would help us.
   b. If she isn't busy, she would help us.
   c. If she weren't busy, she would help us.
   d. If she was busy, she would help us.

9. a. If he is sick, I would call the doctor.
   b. If he were sick, I will call the doctor.
   c. If he was sick, I would call the doctor.
   d. If he were sick, I would call the doctor.

10. a. If it weren't funny, I wouldn't laugh.
    b. If it weren't funny, I won't laugh.
    c. If it wasn't funny, I wouldn't laugh.
    d. If it wasn't funny, I won't laugh.

11. a. If I was you, I would leave now.
    b. If I was you, I will leave now.
    c. If I were you, I would leave now.
    d. If I will be you, I would leave now.

12. a. She was upset if he is late.
    b. She will be upset if he was late.
    c. She were upset if he would be late.
    d. She would be upset if he were late.

I **"CAN-DO" REVIEW**

Match the "can do" statement and the correct sentence.

_____ 1. I can ask for information.

_____ 2. I can say that I don't know something.

_____ 3. I can apologize.

_____ 4. I can express uncertainty.

_____ 5. I can make a suggestion.

_____ 6. I can ask about future plans.

_____ 7. I can ask for advice.

_____ 8. I can express hopes.

_____ 9. I can express agreement.

_____ 10. I can make a deduction.

a. I'm not really sure.

b. The boss must be in a bad mood.

c. Could you tell me what time our plane leaves?

d. What are you going to do this weekend?

e. Do you think I should go to work with this cold?

f. You're right.

g. I'm sorry.

h. Why don't you check with the librarian?

i. I don't know when my car will be fixed.

j. I hope the economy improves next year.

A WHAT'S THE WORD?

1. I think the children _____ scared if the lights went out.
   a. will be
   b. would be *(circled)*

2. I think your parents would be angry if you _____ school tomorrow.
   a. skipped
   b. skip

3. I think Jim would be disappointed if I _____ his party.
   a. was missing
   b. missed

4. Do you think I would be happier if I _____ rich?
   a. was
   b. were

5. I think the children would be excited if it _____.
   a. snowed
   b. snows

6. I think the neighbors _____ annoyed if I practiced the drums now.
   a. would be
   b. are going to be

7. I think this pizza would be better if it _____ more cheese on it.
   a. have
   b. had

8. I think we would be unhappy if our teacher _____ a test today.
   a. gave
   b. gives

9. Do you think Bob _____ jealous if I got into law school?
   a. would be
   b. is going to be

10. I think my sister would be upset if I _____ her new computer.
    a. use
    b. used

B IF

1. I know I would be scared if a robber *(be)* ___were___ in my house.

2. Do you think Amy would be jealous if I *(go out)* _____ with her boyfriend?

3. I'm sure I would be concerned if I *(get lost)* _____ in New York City.

4. I'm positive Johnny would be upset if he *(have)* _____ the flu on his birthday.

5. I know that my doctor would be pleased if I *(eat)* _____ healthier foods.

6. I'd be very upset if I *(lose)* _____ the keys to my car.

7. My wife would be upset if I *(quit)* _____ my job.

8. All the neighbors would be unhappy if the landlord *(sell)* _____ our apartment building.

1. A. Do you think Mom would be happy if I ....
   ....?

   B. Of course _____she would_____. _____She'd be_____
   very happy. That's a wonderful idea.

2. A. Do you think Dad would be angry if I ....
   ....?

   B. I'm sure _____. _____
   very angry. That's a terrible idea.

3. A. Do you think the boss would be pleased if I ....
   ....?

   B. I'm positive _____. _____
   very pleased.

4. A. Do you think our grandchildren would be disappointed if we
   ....?

   B. Of course _____. _____
   very disappointed.

5. A. Do you think our teacher would be annoyed if we ....
   ....?

   B. I'm afraid _____. _____
   very annoyed.

6. A. Do you think my wife would be upset if I ....
   ....?

   B. Of course _____. _____
   very upset.

1. If I _____ you, I wouldn't miss Grandma's birthday party.
   a. was
   (b.) were

2. If you _____ a gallon of ice cream, you'd probably feel sick.
   a. ate
   b. eat

3. If you always practiced the guitar at two in the morning, I'm sure _____ evicted from your building.
   a. you'll be
   b. you'd be

4. If I were you, _____ your children to play a musical instrument.
   a. I encourage
   b. I'd encourage

5. If you _____ at the meeting late, you'd probably be embarrassed.
   a. arrived
   b. arrive

6. If I _____ the money, I would definitely buy a better car.
   a. have
   b. had

7. If today were Saturday, _____ until noon.
   a. I'd sleep
   b. I'll sleep

8. If the mayor raised taxes, people _____ vote for him in the next election.
   a. won't
   b. wouldn't

9. If he _____ me more often, I'd be very pleased.
   a. visits
   b. visited

10. To tell the truth, I _____ the phone if I were you.
    a. wouldn't answer
    b. won't answer

11. If you said you could come home tomorrow, _____ very happy.
    a. we're
    b. we'd be

12. If our teacher _____ easier, I'm sure I'd get better grades.
    a. was
    b. were

E **LISTENING**

Listen and complete the sentences.

1. a. . . . you'll look very old.
   (b.) . . . you'd look very old.

2. a. . . . I'll call you.
   b. . . . I'd call you.

3. a. . . . you'll probably get carsick.
   b. . . . you'd probably get carsick.

4. a. . . . I'll clean my yard.
   b. . . . I'd clean my yard.

5. a. . . . he'll be upset.
   b. . . . he'd probably be upset.

6. a. . . . you'll be very cold.
   b. . . . you'd be very cold.

7. a. . . . I won't be very happy.
   b. . . . I'm not very happy.

8. a. . . . you'll probably regret it.
   b. . . . you'd probably regret it.

9. a. . . . you'll miss something important.
   b. . . . you miss something important.

10. a. . . . you'll probably lose your shirt.
    b. . . . you'd probably lose your shirt.

11. a. . . . I'd call the landlord.
    b. . . . I'll call the landlord.

12. a. . . . you'd be very sorry.
    b. . . . you'll be very sorry.

1. A. I'm thinking of going skating this afternoon.

   B. I wouldn't go skating this afternoon if I were you. It's very

   warm. If you ___went___ skating today, ___you'd___

   probably ___fall___ into the pond.

2. A. I'm thinking of tuning up my car myself.

   B. I wouldn't do that. If I were you, _____ call Charlie,

   the mechanic. _____ definitely _____

   _____ correctly.

3. A. I'm thinking of going to the prom with Larry.

   B. You are?! I wouldn't do that if I were you. If you _____

   to the prom with Larry, _____ probably _____
   a terrible time.

4. A. I'm thinking of painting my house red.

   B. Really? I wouldn't paint it red if I were you. If

   _____ your house red, _____
   look awful!

5. A. I'm thinking of driving downtown this morning.

   B. I _____ downtown if I were you. If

   _____ downtown, _____ probably get stuck
   in a lot of traffic.

6. A. I'm thinking of having a party this weekend while my parents
      are away.

   B. I _____ a party if I were you. If _____

   _____ a party, I'm sure your parents _____
   very upset.

(continued)

7. A. I'm thinking of seeing the new Julie Richards movie this weekend.

B. To tell the truth, I _____ it if I were you.

It's terrible! If _____ it, _____ probably be very bored.

8. A. I'm thinking of buying a parrot.

B. I wouldn't buy a parrot if I _____ you. If _____ _____ a parrot, _____ make a lot of noise!

9. A. I'm thinking of ....

B. I wouldn't ....

If ....,

....

G **GRAMMARRAP:** *If I Were You* 🔊

Listen. Then clap and practice.

A. What color · do you think · I should paint · my house?

B.   If I · were you, · I'd paint it · blue.

A. What time · do you think · I should leave · for the plane?

B.   If I · were you, · I'd leave · at two.

A. What food · do you think · I should serve · my guests?

B.   If I · were you, · I'd serve them · stew.

A.   Where · do you think · I should go · with my kids?

B.   If I · were you, · I'd go · to the zoo.

H WHAT DO THEY WISH?

1. The Johnson family has a small car. They wish they _____ a larger one.
   a. have
   b.) had

2. I work the night shift at the factory. I wish I _____ the day shift.
   a. worked
   b. work

3. I'm disappointed with my new haircut. I _____ it weren't so short.
   a. wish
   b. wished

4. Barbara has two children. She wishes she _____ three.
   a. has
   b. had

5. I always forget to check the messages on my answering machine. I wish I _____ to check them.
   a. remembered
   b. remember

6. My boyfriend is a cook. He _____ he were a mechanic.
   a. wishes
   b. wished

7. I'm sick and tired of working. I wish I _____ on vacation.
   a. was
   b. were

8. I live in Minnesota, but I wish I _____ in Florida.
   a. live
   b. lived

9. I send e-mails to my girlfriend every day. I wish she _____ back to me.
   a. wrote
   b. writes

10. I enjoy making big holiday meals for my family. I wish I _____ washing the dishes, too.
    a. enjoy
    b. enjoyed

I LISTENING

Listen and complete the conversations.

1. a. . . . it is.
   b.) . . . it were.

2. a. . . . you talk more.
   b. . . . you talked less.

3. a. . . . it were easier.
   b. . . . I were easier.

4. a. . . . he daydreams more.
   b. . . . he daydreamed less.

5. a. . . . they're scarier.
   b. . . . they were scarier.

6. a. . . . you sang more softly.
   b. . . . you sing softly.

7. a. . . . it has e-mail.
   b. . . . it had e-mail.

8. a. . . . I worked near my house.
   b. . . . I work near my house.

9. a. . . . I was married.
   b. . . . I were married.

10. a. . . . it were larger.
    b. . . . it was smaller.

11. a. . . . he is working.
    b. . . . he were working.

12. a. . . . you called more often.
    b. . . . you call more often.

J I WISH

1. _____I wish I felt_____ better today. I really don't feel well at all.

2. _____ it _____. When it's 5:00, I can leave work.

3. _____ as well as my sister does. She has a magnificent voice.

4. _____ history. Teaching history is much more interesting than teaching driver's ed.

5. _____ our teacher _____ us less homework. She gives us a lot of homework every day.

6. _____. I think dogs are the best pets in the world.

K YOU DECIDE: *What Does Teddy Wish?*

My friend Teddy isn't very happy. He's never satisfied with anything.

1. Teddy lives in the suburbs. He wishes _____.

2. Teddy's father is a dentist. He wishes _____.

3. His mother teaches English at his school. He wishes _____.

4. Teddy has two older sisters. He wishes _____.

5. Teddy's father drives a used car. He wishes _____.

6. Teddy plays the trombone. _____.

7. A lot of Teddy's friends _____, but Teddy doesn't. He wishes _____

_____.

8. Also, _____. He wishes _____

_____.

A. I wonder if you could help me. I'm looking for a job as a repairperson.

B. Most of the repair shops in town want to hire people who can repair many different kinds of things. For example, can you repair TVs?

A. I wish _____ I could ___¹, but TVs are very complicated.

B. That's too bad. If _____² repair TVs, _____³ able to find a job more easily. Hmm. *Freddy's Fix-It Shop* is looking for someone who can repair DVD players.

A. The truth is, I'm very good at repairing CD players, but I can't repair DVD players.

B. That's too bad! If _____⁴, *Freddy's Fix-It Shop*

_____⁵ VERY interested in you.

A. *Freddy's Fix-It Shop* is one of the best repair shops in town. I wish _____⁶ repair DVD players.

B. Well, *We Fix It!* is also a repair shop, and they're looking for someone who can repair

CD players and _____⁷. They also want someone who can _____

_____⁸.

A. I'm afraid I can't _____⁹.

B. What a shame! If _____¹⁰, *We Fix It!*

_____¹¹ interested in you. Maybe you should think about finding another kind of job. What else can you do?

A. Let's see. I used to be a waiter, but I hurt my back, so I can't do that anymore.

B. I wish you _____¹² be a waiter. If _____¹³ a waiter,

_____¹⁴ any trouble finding a job. There must be other things

you can do. For example, can you _____¹⁵?

A. Not really.

B. That's too bad, because if _____¹⁶,

_____¹⁷ send you for an interview with the _____¹⁸ Company.

I'm sorry, but those are all the jobs I have today. I wish _____¹⁹ help you. Come back next week. Maybe I'll have something then.

1. If the children were asleep, _____ have some peace and quiet in the house.
   a. we'd be able to
   b. we couldn't
   c. we'll

2. If I saw you more often, _____ get to know each other better.
   a. we couldn't
   b. we could
   c. we can

3. If you were more talented, _____ be in the movies.
   a. you'll
   b. you can
   c. you'd be able to

4. If the TV weren't so loud, _____ concentrate on my homework.
   a. I will
   b. I could
   c. I can't

5. If Ms. Evans weren't so busy, _____ speak with her now.
   a. you could
   b. you couldn't
   c. you wouldn't be able to

6. If he didn't live in the suburbs, _____ get to work faster.
   a. he'll
   b. he won't be able to
   c. he could

7. If you had more spare time, _____ learn to knit.
   a. you could
   b. you can
   c. you'll

8. If Ms. Jackson made more money, _____ buy a new computer.
   a. she couldn't
   b. she'd be able to
   c. she can

9. If I were more athletic, _____ play on the school basketball team.
   a. I could
   b. I can
   c. I couldn't

10. If he weren't so clumsy, _____ dance better.
    a. he will
    b. he can't
    c. he'd be able to

N LISTENING

Listen and decide what the person is talking about.

1. a. speaking a language
   b. writing a language

2. a. flowers
   b. vegetables

3. a. my driver's license
   b. a raise

4. a. the bus
   b. school

5. a. food
   b. money

6. a. preparing taxes
   b. watching TV

O YOU DECIDE WHY

A. I'm really annoyed with our neighbors upstairs.

They always .... ,

they always .... ,

and they're ....

B. I know.

I wish _____ ,

I wish _____ ,

and I wish _____ .
We should probably speak to the landlord.

P GRAMMARRAP: *I Wish*

Listen. Then clap and practice.

I wish   I had   a more interesting   job.

I wish   I made   more money.

I wish   I were sitting   and reading   a book.

On a beach   where it's warm   and sunny.

I wish   we lived   on a quiet   street.

I wish   our neighbors   were nice.

I wish   our roof   weren't leaking.

I wish   we didn't   have mice.

I wish   I could be   on a sports team.

I wish   I were six feet   tall.

I wish   I knew how   to play tennis.

I wish   I could throw   a ball.

Activity Workbook   **87**

1. I had trouble answering the questions.
   a. The questions were confusing.
   b. The questions were amusing.
   c. I answered all the questions three times.

2. I'm positive we're having a test tomorrow.
   a. I'm afraid we might have a test.
   b. I'm sure we're having a test.
   c. I think we'll probably have a test.

3. We can't convince him to take the job.
   a. He wants to take the job.
   b. He can't take the job.
   c. He won't take the job.

4. Carl is happy he moved to the suburbs.
   a. He prefers the city.
   b. He likes taking care of his yard.
   c. He likes the noise in the city.

5. Mrs. Randall wants to teach something else.
   a. She wants to teach the same thing again.
   b. She wants to teach at a different time.
   c. She wants to teach a different subject.

6. The Super Bowl is next Sunday. I'm going to invite a friend over to watch it on TV.
   a. I'm thinking about my Super Bowl plans.
   b. I'm having a big Super Bowl party.
   c. I'm going to the Super Bowl.

7. Amy and Dan don't have enough in common.
   a. They don't get paid enough.
   b. They don't have enough clothes.
   c. They aren't interested in the same things.

8. We live in a high-rise building.
   a. Our house is in the mountains.
   b. Our building has many floors.
   c. Our building isn't very large, but the rents are high.

9. Ronald is sick and tired of his job.
   a. He's in the hospital.
   b. He's unhappy.
   c. He's taking medicine.

10. My sister Nancy is never annoyed.
    a. She's never upset.
    b. She's never in a good mood.
    c. She never enjoys anything.

11. My cousin Norman dropped out of school.
    a. He skipped a few classes.
    b. He quit school.
    c. He ran away from school very quickly.

12. Our apartment has a view of the park.
    a. We can see the park from our window.
    b. We can't see the park from our apartment.
    c. We can hear the park very well.

13. I'd like some peace and quiet around the house.
    a. Our house is very quiet.
    b. Our house is very large.
    c. Our house is very noisy.

14. Ever since I heard we were going to have an important exam next week, I've been concentrating on my work.
    a. I've been complaining more about it.
    b. I've been paying more attention to it.
    c. I've been worrying more.

15. I'm afraid your brakes are getting worse.
    a. They need to be replaced.
    b. They need to be rehearsed.
    c. They need to be tuned up.

16. My brother-in-law started a new business, and he lost his shirt.
    a. He's looked everywhere for it.
    b. It was successful.
    c. His business wasn't very successful.

SOUND IT OUT!

Listen to each word and then say it.

| bread | | | break | | |

1. fell   3. eggs   5. pleasure   1. paid   3. ate   5. plays
2. special   4. athletic   6. many   2. space   4. operation   6. main

Listen and put a circle around the word that has the same sound.

1. sweater:	grade	(gets)	parade
2. main:	take	let	terrible
3. ready:	away	great	Ted
4. operation:	upset	paid	pepper
5. paint:	rest	vacation	said
6. complain:	then	said	Spain
7. spend:	sprain	Jane	when
8. tell:	friend	weigh	receive

Now make a sentence using all the words you circled, and read the sentence aloud.

9. .... my ...., he'll
.... a .... in ....

10. toothpaste:	best	play	past
11. hate:	hat	eight	head
12. special:	tennis	came	cat
13. lesson:	late	great	let's
14. upset:	skate	made	next
15. pleasure:	mail	Wednesday	plane
16. friend:	Fred	wait	same

Now make a sentence using all the words you circled, and read the sentence aloud.

17. .... with ....
at .... o'clock.

A WHAT'S THE ANSWER?

1. Alan didn't tell his mother he had a bad cold last week. If _____, she would have made him chicken soup.
   a. he had told her
   b. he told her

2. Ron wasn't prepared for his English test. If _____ for it, he would have gotten a better grade.
   a. he had been prepared
   b. he was prepared

3. Mrs. Vickers didn't get paid today. If she had gotten paid, she _____ her family out to dinner at a nice retaurant.
   a. wouldn't have taken
   b. would have taken

4. Debbie didn't have time to finish her homework. If _____, she would have finished it.
   a. she had time
   b. she had had time

5. Margaret didn't answer her phone. If she had answered it, she _____ about her brother's engagement.
   a. would have known
   b. would know

6. I didn't go to the meeting this morning because I didn't know about it. If _____ about it, I would have gone.
   a. I knew
   b. I had known

7. Luckily, Ted didn't get stuck in traffic. If he had been stuck in traffic, _____ his plane.
   a. he would have missed
   b. he would miss

8. Greta didn't go to work yesterday because she wasn't feeling well. If she had been feeling well, _____ to work.
   a. she would go
   b. she would have gone

9. Mr. and Mrs. Davis didn't have good seats at the play last night. If _____ good seats, they would have enjoyed it.
   a. they had had
   b. they had

10. My father wasn't in a good mood this afternoon. If he had been in a good mood, _____ baseball with me.
    a. he would have played
    b. he would play

B COMPLETE THE SENTENCES

1. Mr. and Mrs. Fay weren't able to buy the house they wanted because their mortgage wasn't

   approved. If their mortgage __had been approved__, they __would have been able__ to buy
   the house.

2. Mandy didn't arrive on time for school today because her alarm clock didn't ring. If her

   alarm clock _____, she _____ on time.

3. Sam wasn't happy because he didn't win the tennis game.

   If he _____ the tennis game, he _____ happy.

4. My friends didn't get dressed up because they didn't know about the party. If they

   _____ about the party, they _____ dressed up.

5. My daughter didn't learn to play the piano well because she didn't practice every day.

   If she _____ every day, she _____ to play the piano well.

6. We weren't on time for the wedding because we didn't take our map with us.

   If we _____ our map with us, we _____ on time.

7. Cindy didn't stop at the traffic light because she didn't notice it.

   If she _____ it, she definitely _____.

8. We didn't have good seats for the concert because we didn't buy our tickets early enough.

   If we _____ our tickets early enough, we _____ good seats.

C YOU DECIDE: *What Would Happen If . . . ?*

1. I had a terrible time on my vacation!

   The weather wasn't _____ warm enough _____,

   I didn't take _____,

   I wasn't able to _____,

   the hotel didn't have _____,

   _____ weren't _____,

   and _____ didn't write to me while I was away.

   If the weather _____ had been warmer _____,

   if I _____,

   if I _____,

   if the hotel _____,

   if _____,

   and if _____ while I was away,

   I'm sure I _____ would have enjoyed _____ my vacation.

(continued)

2. I had a terrible job interview yesterday at the Trans-Tel Company. I didn't get the job, and I know why.

I didn't remember to ....,

I didn't arrive ....,

I didn't ....,

I wasn't ....,

and I wasn't ....

If I _____,

if I _____,

if I _____,

if I _____,

and if I _____,

I'm sure I _____ a better job interview.

And if I _____ a better job interview,

maybe I _____ the job.

3. I didn't enjoy myself at my cousin's birthday party last night.

The music wasn't ....,

the food wasn't ....,

the people there weren't ....,

.... wasn't ....,

and .... didn't ....

If the music _____,

if the food _____,

if the people there _____,

if _____,

and if _____,

I'm sure I _____ myself at the party.

WHAT'S THE ANSWER?

1. If I hadn't expected Maria to say "yes,"
   I _____ her to marry me.
   a. wouldn't have asked
   b. wouldn't ask

2. If you hadn't set off the metal detector,
   you _____ searched.
   a. wouldn't get
   b. wouldn't have gotten

3. If Janet's mortgage _____ approved, she
   wouldn't have been able to buy a house.
   a. hadn't been
   b. wasn't

4. If I _____ problems with my printer
   last night, I wouldn't have turned in my
   paper late.
   a. didn't have
   b. hadn't had

5. If Timmy's report card _____ bad, his
   parents wouldn't have been upset.
   a. hadn't been
   b. wasn't

6. If we hadn't felt under the weather,
   we _____ home.
   a. didn't stay
   b. wouldn't have stayed

7. If Debbie _____ her leg, she wouldn't
   have missed the class trip.
   a. didn't sprain
   b. hadn't sprained

8. If the boss hadn't been upset, he _____
   at everybody this morning.
   a. wouldn't have yelled
   b. wouldn't yell

9. If it _____ cold last week, there
   wouldn't have been ice on the pond.
   a. wasn't
   b. hadn't been

10. If I hadn't had a bad headache, I _____
    to bed so early.
    a. wouldn't go
    b. wouldn't have gone

E **LISTENING** 🔊

Listen and choose the statement that is true based on what you hear.

1. a. She got the job.
   b. She didn't speak confidently.

2. a. He got fired.
   b. He arrived on time for work every
      day.

3. a. It rained.
   b. They didn't have to cancel the picnic.

4. a. He wasn't in a hurry.
   b. He made mistakes on his homework.

5. a. She didn't call them.
   b. She remembered their phone number.

6. a. The play wasn't boring.
   b. The audience fell asleep.

7. a. They weren't in the mood to go
      swimming.
   b. They went to the beach.

8. a. He didn't get a ticket.
   b. He was speeding.

9. a. She didn't write legibly.
   b. She wrote legibly.

10. a. He remembered the meeting.
    b. He didn't go to the meeting.

HOW I BECAME A BASKETBALL PLAYER

A. Why did you decide to become a basketball player?

B. When I was very young, my uncle took me to basketball games every weekend, my grandparents bought me a basketball, and my parents sent me to basketball camp. When I was older, I played basketball in high school and college, and I went to basketball games whenever I could.

If my uncle _____hadn't taken me___¹ to basketball games every weekend,

if my grandparents _____² a basketball,

if my parents _____³ to basketball camp,

if I _____⁴ basketball in high school and college,

and if I _____⁵ to basketball games whenever I could,

I _____wouldn't have become_____⁶ a basketball player.

I'M REALLY GLAD

I'm really glad I went to Five-Star Business School.

If _____I hadn't gone_____¹ to Five-Star,

I _____wouldn't have_____² learned information technology.

And if I _____³ information technology,

I _____⁴ a job at the Trans-Tel Company.

And if I_____⁵ a job at Trans-Tel,

I _____⁶ sent to Vancouver on business.

And if I _____⁷ sent to Vancouver on business,

I _____⁸ met your father.

And if I _____⁹ your father,

you _____¹⁰ born!

WHY DIDN'T YOU TELL ME?

Why didn't you tell me today's English class was canceled? If _____you had told_____ [1]

me it was canceled, I _____ [2] to school this morning. And

if I _____ [3] to school, I _____ [4] here when the

repairperson came to pick up the computer. And if _____ [5] here when the

repairperson came to pick it up, she _____ [6] able to take it to her

repair shop. And if she _____ [7] able to take it to her shop, I'm sure she

_____ [8] fixed it. And if she _____ [9] it, we would be on the

Internet right now!

Why didn't you tell me you had invited your friends for dinner last night? If you

_____ [10] me you had invited them, I definitely would have _____ [11]

more food. If I _____ [12] more food, there would have been enough for

everyone to eat. And if _____ [13] enough food for everybody to eat, we

_____ [14] to Ziggy's Restaurant for dinner. And if we _____

_____ [15] to Ziggy's for dinner, we _____ [16] sick.

And if we _____ [17] sick, we _____ [18] had to go to the hospital.

And if we _____ [19] to go to the hospital, we _____ [20]

home, and you could _____ [21] your homework. And if you _____ [22]

your homework, your teacher _____ [23] upset.

YOU DECIDE: *Why Was Larry Late for Work?*

I'm sorry I was late for work this morning. I tried to get here on time, but everything went wrong.

First, ...

Then, ...

After that, ...

And also, ...

If _____ ,

if _____ ,

if _____ ,

and if _____ ,

I _____ so late.

GRAMMARRAP: *If They Hadn't*

Listen. Then clap and practice.

If he hadn't   been asked   to dance   in the show,

He wouldn't have   slipped   and broken   his toe.

If she hadn't   decided   to learn   to ski,

She wouldn't   have fallen   and hurt   her knee.

If you hadn't   lost   the keys   to your car,

You wouldn't have   had   to walk   so far.

If we hadn't   left   our tickets   at home,

We wouldn't have   missed   the flight   to Rome.

K WHAT'S THE ANSWER?

1. Henry didn't enjoy the lecture. He wishes _____ home.
   a. he stayed
   b. he had stayed *(circled)*

2. I don't do my homework all the time. My teacher wishes _____.
   a. I did
   b. I had done

3. When I was young, I used to feel bad because I wasn't as athletic as the other students in my class. I wish _____ athletic.
   a. I was
   b. I had been

4. When we moved into this neighborhood, we were invited to a big neighborhood party. We wish _____.
   a. we had gone
   b. we went

5. We don't know if it's a girl or a boy. We wish _____.
   a. we knew
   b. we had known

6. I didn't read the instructions very carefully. I wish _____ them more carefully.
   a. I read
   b. I had read

7. My parents always worry about the future when they hear bad news on TV. I wish _____ so much.
   a. they hadn't worried
   b. they didn't worry

8. Mrs. Watson is concerned that her husband doesn't eat better food. She wishes _____ healthier things.
   a. he ate
   b. he had eaten

L COMPLETE THE SENTENCES

1. I'm a terrible dancer. I wish _____ I had taken _____ dance lessons when I was younger.

2. Amy didn't study for her math test, and she got a bad grade. She wishes _____ _____ for it.

3. Fred doesn't enjoy working in the Accounting Department. He wishes _____ in the Personnel Department.

4. I love dogs. I wish _____ a dog when I was young. My mother didn't like dogs. She liked cats. We had five of them!

5. When my friends go skiing, I never go with them because I can't ski. I wish _____ how to ski.

6. I'm really sorry I didn't see the new James Bond movie when it was playing downtown last month. I wish _____ it.

7. My wife and I are both being transferred to our company's office on the east coast, and now we have to sell our house. We wish _____ sell it.

PATTY'S PARTY

These people didn't have a very good time at Patty's party last night.

1. I didn't have a very good time at Patty's party last night. I wish I ___hadn't___ ___gone___. There were a lot of other things I could have done. I wish I _____ _____ something else.

2. Patty's party was outside, and it was very cold. If it _____ _____ so cold, I _____ _____ _____ more comfortable.

3. I'm very sorry that Claudia Crandall was at the party. She didn't stop singing and playing the guitar. I CERTAINLY wish she _____ _____ and _____ the guitar. She has the worst voice I've ever heard, and she plays the guitar VERY badly. If Claudia _____ _____ and _____ the guitar at the party, I _____ _____ _____ a headache all night!

4. I wish I _____ forget people's names all the time. Can you believe it? I couldn't remember Patty's sister's name. I wish I _____ _____ it. After all, if she _____ forgotten MY name, I _____ _____ liked it.

5. I wish I _____ _____ more people at the party. I didn't know anybody at all. If I _____ _____ more people, I _____ _____ _____ so lonely, and I _____ _____ _____ so out of place.

Listen. Then clap and practice.

I wish   I hadn't skied   down the mountain.
I wish   I had watched   TV.
If I hadn't   skied   down the mountain,
I wouldn't have   hurt   my knee.

I wish   I hadn't walked   to the office.
I wish   I had taken   the train.
If I hadn't   walked   to the office,
I wouldn't have gotten   caught   in the rain.

I wish   I hadn't typed   so carelessly.
I wish   I had done   much better.
If I hadn't   typed   so carelessly,
I wouldn't have had to redo   this letter.

I wish   I hadn't swum   in the ocean.
I wish   I had gone   to the park.
If I hadn't   swum   in the ocean,
I wouldn't have gotten   scared   by a shark.

I wish   I hadn't used   so much toothpaste.
I wish   I had used   much less.
If I hadn't   used   so much toothpaste,
I wouldn't have   made   such a mess.

O HOPES AND WISHES

1. A. I heard that I might get a promotion. Can you tell me if it's true?

   B. I wish I _____could tell_____ you now, but I'm not supposed to say anything. I hope I _____can tell_____ you soon.

2. A. Do you like your job?

   B. My job is very boring. I wish I _____ someplace else. I'm looking for a job at an Internet company. I hope I _____ one soon.

3. A. I wish Ricardo Palermo _____ "Loving You" last night. He's the most fantastic singer I've ever heard.

   B. I certainly hope he _____ it when I go to his concert on Saturday night.

4. A. I'm having trouble learning to speak English. I'm afraid I'm too old. I wish I _____ English when I was younger.

   B. Don't be ridiculous! You do a lot better than many of the younger students in our class. They all wish they _____ English as well as you.

5. A. I wish you _____ have to leave on a business trip. I'm really going to miss you. I hope you _____ a good time while you're away, but don't enjoy yourself TOO much!

   B. You know I'm going to miss you, too. I wish you _____ going with me.

6. A. I had my yearly check-up today, and my doctor is a little concerned about my weight.

   B. What did the doctor say?

   A. He wishes I _____ so heavy. He gave me a new diet that I'm going to try. I hope I _____ a lot of weight.

YOU DECIDE: *If*

1. I hope it doesn't rain this weekend. If it rains this weekend, ...

....

2. I wish I had more free time. If I had more free time, ...

....

3. I wish I didn't have to .... If I didn't have to

.... , ...

4. I hope you can lend me .... If you can lend me

.... , ...

5. I wish I had .... many years ago. If I had ....

.... , ...

6. I hope .... is elected president. If .... is elected president,

....

7. I wish I knew more about .... If I knew more about

.... , ...

8. I hope .... in the future. If ....

.... , ...

Q **WISH OR HOPE?**

1. They ((wish)   hope) they had taken their umbrellas today.

2. Timothy can't drive yet. He (wishes   hopes) he were older.

3. I (wish   hope) I find the right ingredients for the soup.

4. Mrs. Jones (wishes   hopes) her son hadn't quit the baseball team.

5. John (wishes   hopes) his shirt doesn't shrink in the washing machine.

6. I (wish   hope) I didn't have to wait so long to see if I got accepted to college.

7. Tomorrow is Saturday. I (wish   hope) I still don't feel "under the weather."

8. Mr. McDonald doesn't like his new house. He (wishes   hopes) he had bought a condominium.

9. The minister is embarrassed. He (wishes   hopes) he hadn't arrived late for the wedding.

LISTENING

Listen and complete the sentences.

1. a. . . . I wouldn't be so nervous.
   b. . . . I won't be so irritable.

2. a. . . . I'll be home right away.
   b. . . . I wouldn't be late.

3. a. . . . he'll have a lot more friends.
   b. . . . he'd be a lot happier.

4. a. . . . she wouldn't have gotten wet.
   b. . . . she'll be dry.

5. a. . . . we'd dance together.
   b. . . . we'll talk to each other all evening.

6. a. . . . I won't have to walk to work.
   b. . . . I wouldn't have to drive everywhere.

S **LISTENING:** *Hopes and Wishes*

Listen and complete the sentences.

1. a. . . . he isn't sick.
   b. . . . he felt better.

2. a. . . . tomorrow's lesson is easier.
   b. . . . I understood English better.

3. a. . . . she visits me more often.
   b. . . . she still lived across the street.

4. a. . . . she can't work someplace else.
   b. . . . she can find another job.

5. a. . . . I had a dog or a cat.
   b. . . . I can get a pet.

6. a. . . . I'm a more graceful dancer.
   b. . . . I weren't so clumsy.

7. a. . . . you can come.
   b. . . . you could be there.

8. a. . . . she were more careful.
   b. . . . she finds it soon.

9. a. . . . they tasted good.
   b. . . . everybody likes chocolate.

10. a. . . . it were healthier.
    b. . . . it needs more sun.

11. a. . . . you knew more about fax machines.
    b. . . . you know how to fix it.

12. a. . . . she owned a more reliable car.
    b. . . . it starts on cold days.

13. a. . . . I had some.
    b. . . . we can borrow some.

14. a. . . . I had a better memory.
    b. . . . I can remember them.

T **LISTENING**

Listen to each word and then say it.

1. beg—bay

2. check—shake

3. Fred—afraid

4. men—Main

5. met—made

6. never—neighbor

7. pepper—paper

8. set—say

9. pet—paid

10. wedding—waiting

Listen and complete the sentences.

| met | made |

1. a. . . . all the beds.
   (b.) . . . an old friend.

| fell | fail |

2. a. . . . while they were skiing.
   b. . . . whenever they take a test.

| teller | tailor |

3. a. . . . works in a bank.
   b. . . . takes in your clothes.

| pepper | paper |

4. a. . . . in my notebook.
   b. . . . in the stew.

| Fred | afraid |

5. a. . . . you might drown?
   b. . . . Smith?

| met | made |

6. a. . . . any summer plans yet?
   b. . . . their new neighbors?

| men | Main |

7. a. . . . Street bus is leaving.
   b. . . . are leaving the barber shop.

| check | shake |

8. a. . . . hands.
   b. . . . with the mechanic.

| wedding | waiting |

9. a. . . . at the bus stop.
   b. . . . was the happiest day of my life.

| never | neighbor |

10. a. . . . just moved in yesterday.
    b. . . . flown in a helicopter before.

| pet | paid |

11. a. . . . her income tax.
    b. . . . bird knows how to talk.

| check | shake |

12. a. . . . hands with the ticket agent.
    b. . . . with the ticket agent.

| fell | fail |

13. a. . . . most of my English exams.
    b. . . . asleep very late last night.

| wedding | waiting |

14. a. . . . for us.
    b. . . . is at 11:00.

| never | neighbor |

15. a. . . . is very noisy.
    b. . . . been to Hawaii.

| Fred | afraid |

16. a. . . . I'll get hurt.
    b. . . . Jones. What's your name?

WHAT DID THEY SAY?

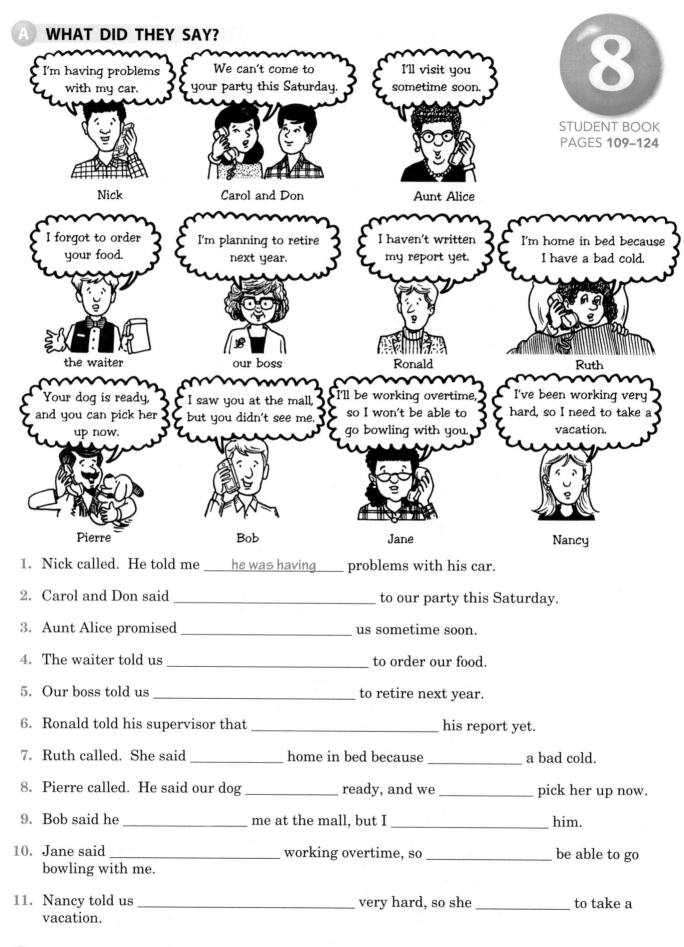

8

1. Nick called. He told me ____he was having____ problems with his car.

2. Carol and Don said _____ to our party this Saturday.

3. Aunt Alice promised _____ us sometime soon.

4. The waiter told us _____ to order our food.

5. Our boss told us _____ to retire next year.

6. Ronald told his supervisor that _____ his report yet.

7. Ruth called. She said _____ home in bed because _____ a bad cold.

8. Pierre called. He said our dog _____ ready, and we _____ pick her up now.

9. Bob said he _____ me at the mall, but I _____ him.

10. Jane said _____ working overtime, so _____ be able to go bowling with me.

11. Nancy told us _____ very hard, so she _____ to take a vacation.

B MESSAGES

1.

Dear Mother,
I got an "A" on my biology test.
                              Love,
                              Amy

A. I just got an e-mail from my daughter in college.

B. Really? What did she say?

A. She said _____ she had gotten an "A"

_____ on her biology test _____.

2.

A. I received a note from Uncle Ralph today.

B. Oh, that's nice. What did he say?

A. He said _____

_____.

Dear Gloria,
I'm home from the hospital and I'm feeling much better.
                              Uncle Ralph

3.

Dear Sue and Mike,
We saw the Colosseum, but we haven't gone to the Vatican yet.
                The Wilsons

A. The Wilsons sent us a postcard from Rome.

B. Oh, really? What did they say?

A. They said _____

_____.

4.

A. I got an e-mail from my friend Richard today.

B. He hasn't written in a while. What did he say?

A. He said _____

_____.

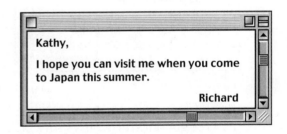

Kathy,
I hope you can visit me when you come to Japan this summer.
                              Richard

5.

Dear Mr. Watson,
I'm sorry, but you aren't the right person for the job.
Sincerely,
Roberta Bennett

A. I received an e-mail from Ms. Bennett at the Apex Company.

B. Oh. You've been expecting her to write. What did she say?

A. She said _____

_____.

(continued)

6. A. Charlie, the plumber, left us a note.

B. Oh. What did he say?

A. He said _____

_____.

Dear Mr. and Mrs. Blake,

I'm very busy, and I can't repair your dishwasher this week.

Charlie

7.

Hi everyone!

We love Hawaii, and we're thinking of buying a condominium.

Love,
Grandma & Grandpa

A. We received a postcard from Grandma and Grandpa in Hawaii.

B. That's nice. Are they enjoying their vacation there?

A. Yes. They said _____

_____.

8. A. I received an e-mail from my father last night.

B. What did he say?

A. He said _____

_____

_____.

Dear Brian,

I was hoping to send you more money for college, but I won't be able to because I'm having financial problems.

Dad

9.

Dear Ann and Tom,

I'll be arriving ....

and I plan to ....

....

A. We received a note from Cousin George.

B. Oh. What did he say?

A. He said _____

_____.

10. A. We got a letter from Aunt Clara today.

B. That's nice. What did she say?

A. She said _____

_____

_____.

Dear ....,

I have some good news.

I'm finally going to ....

....

....

11.

Dear ....,
You won't believe it, but ....
....
....

A. I received an e-mail from my friend Larry.

B. He hasn't written in a long time. What did he say?

A. He said _____

_____

_____.

GRAMMARRAP: *What Did They Say?*

Listen. Then clap and practice.

A. What did he say?
B. He said he was mad.
A. What did she say?
B. She said she was sad.

A. What did she say?
B. She said she was busy.
A. What did he say?
B. He said he was dizzy.

A. What did she say?
B. She said she'd been hired.
A. What did he say?
B. He said he'd been fired.

A. What did they say?
B. They said they'd be late.
A. What did you say?
B. We said we would wait.

D WHAT'S THE ANSWER?

1. A. We can't fish here.
   B. Really? I was sure _____ fish here.
   a. we can
   b. we could *(circled)*

2. A. My husband wants to sell our house.
   B. Oh. I didn't know _____ to sell it.
   a. he wanted
   b. he had wanted

3. A. Has the meeting been canceled?
   B. I thought everybody knew it _____.
   a. was canceled
   b. had been canceled

4. A. Susan got a big promotion.
   B. That's nice. I didn't know _____ a promotion.
   a. she had gotten
   b. she got

5. A. My parents have moved to Miami.
   B. Yes. I knew _____ there.
   a. they moved
   b. they had moved

6. A. Our big sale starts tomorrow.
   B. Really? I didn't know _____ tomorrow.
   a. it starts
   b. it started

7. A. Do we have to work overtime today?
   B. I thought everybody knew _____.
   a. we had to work overtime
   b. we have to work overtime

8. A. The school picnic is going to be canceled.
   B. You're kidding! I didn't know the school picnic _____ to be canceled.
   a. was going
   b. is going

E LISTENING

What did they say? Listen and choose the correct answer.

1. a. He said he had fixed their car last week.
   b. He said he could fix their car next week. *(circled)*

2. a. She said her daughter was going to have a baby in July.
   b. She said her daughter had had a baby in July.

3. a. He said that the meeting had been canceled.
   b. He said the meeting was important.

4. a. He said his wife was going to be promoted.
   b. He said his wife had been promoted.

5. a. She said she didn't believe the bus drivers were going on strike.
   b. She said she didn't know the bus drivers.

6. a. He said they had loved each other.
   b. He said they loved each other.

7. a. She said the monkeys had escaped from the zoo.
   b. She said she hadn't believed the monkeys would escape from the zoo.

8. a. He said he was nervous about his interview.
   b. He said he had been nervous about his interview.

9. a. She said her parents had sold their condominium and moved into a house.
   b. She said that her parents had sold their house.

10. a. She said she was going to quit her job.
    b. She said she had moved to Hollywood.

F   YOU DECIDE: *What Happened While Paula Wilson Was Away?*

Paula Wilson just returned home after working in Australia for two years. She's talking to her old friend Steve.

A. Welcome home, Paula! I'm glad you're back. How have you been?

B. Fine. Tell me, what's happened since I've been away?

A. Well, your cousin Frank got married last month.

B. He did? I didn't know _____*he had gotten married*_____¹ last month.
I wonder why he didn't write me.

A. He probably thought you knew. Have you heard about Aunt Martha? She's in the hospital.

B. Really? I had no idea _____². What happened? Did
she have an accident?

A. No. Actually, she had a third heart attack last week.

B. That's terrible! I knew _____³ having problems with her heart for

the past several years, but I didn't know she _____⁴ another heart attack.
I hope she's okay. Tell me, how's your sister Eileen?

A. You probably haven't heard. She's going to become the president of her company next month.

B. That's wonderful! I knew she _____⁵ promoted many times, but I didn't know

she _____⁶ the president of her company! That's very exciting
news. And how are your children?

A. They've been doing very well. My son _____⁷,

and my daughter _____⁸.

B. That's fantastic! I didn't know that your son _____⁹

and your daughter _____¹⁰.

A. By the way, have you heard about Nancy and Tom? They _____

_____¹¹.

B. Really? I had no idea _____¹².
A lot sure has happened recently!

YOU WON'T BELIEVE IT!

Do you like being old?

1. My daughter asked me _____!
   a. do I like being old
   (b.) if I liked being old

2. My students asked me _____.
   a. why the test had been difficult
   b. why was the test so difficult

3. My dentist asked me _____.
   a. whether I ever brushed my teeth
   b. if do I ever brush my teeth

4. My boss asked me what time _____.
   a. did I go to bed last night
   b. I had gone to bed last night

5. My neighbor asked me _____.
   a. if I would sell him my car
   b. if will I sell him my car

6. The job interviewer asked me _____.
   a. where I had learned to spell
   b. where did I learn to spell

7. The salesperson in the store asked me _____!
   a. how old are you
   b. how old I was

8. My girlfriend asked me _____.
   a. if we could get married next month
   b. whether could we get married next month

9. My employees asked me _____.
   a. when was I going to give them raises
   b. when I was going to give them raises

10. My daughter's boyfriend asked me _____.
    a. if I dyed my hair
    b. do I dye my hair

H **LISTENING**

Listen and choose the correct answer.

1. Patty's father asked her _____.
   a. did she break up with Gary
   (b.) if she had broken up with Gary
   c. whether she had broken up with Larry

2. She asked them _____.
   a. how long they had been swimming there
   b. how long had they been sitting there
   c. how long they had been sitting there

3. He asked her _____.
   a. if was she eating when they called
   b. whether she was eating when they called
   c. if she had been reading when they called

4. She asked him _____.
   a. when was he going to repaint it
   b. when he was going to repaint it
   c. if he was going to repair it

5. He asked her _____.
   a. whether she was still sad
   b. if was she still mad
   c. if she was still mad

6. She asked him _____.
   a. when he was going to take a bath
   b. when he was going to study math
   c. if he had studied math

7. He asked me _____.
   a. were they too tall
   b. if they were too tall
   c. whether they were too small

8. She asked him _____.
   a. who had fixed the kitchen floor
   b. who had fixed the kitchen door
   c. who was going to fix the kitchen floor

I WHAT DID THEY ASK?

1. **Have you delivered my letter to Santa Claus yet?**

   A. What did your daughter ask the mail carrier?

   B. She asked him ____(if/whether) he had delivered____
      ____her letter to Santa Claus yet____.

2. **How much time did you spend on your homework?**

   A. Your history teacher looked a little upset after class today.

   B. I know. He asked me _____
      _____.

3. **Can I have another piece of your delicious cake?**

   A. Robert looks very pleased.

   B. He is. His girlfriend asked him _____
      _____.

4. **Why do you always make so much noise?**

   A. I think the Bakers' landlord was upset with them.

   B. He was. He asked them _____
      _____.

5. **Will the operation hurt?**

   A. Was Shirley nervous before her operation?

   B. Yes, she was. She asked the doctor _____
      _____.

(continued)

6.

When is the lecture going to end?

A. George looks bored. What did he just ask his wife?

B. He asked her _____

_____.

7.

Do you still love me?

A. How did Alan feel when he bumped into his former girlfriend?

B. He was VERY surprised. She asked him _____

_____.

8.

Why are there so many grammar rules in English?

A. The students in your class look confused.

B. I know. They asked me _____

_____.

9.

A. Your parents look very concerned. What did they ask you?

B. They asked me _____

_____.

10.

A. Your boss looks very upset. What did she ask you?

B. She asked me _____

_____.

Listen. Then clap and practice.

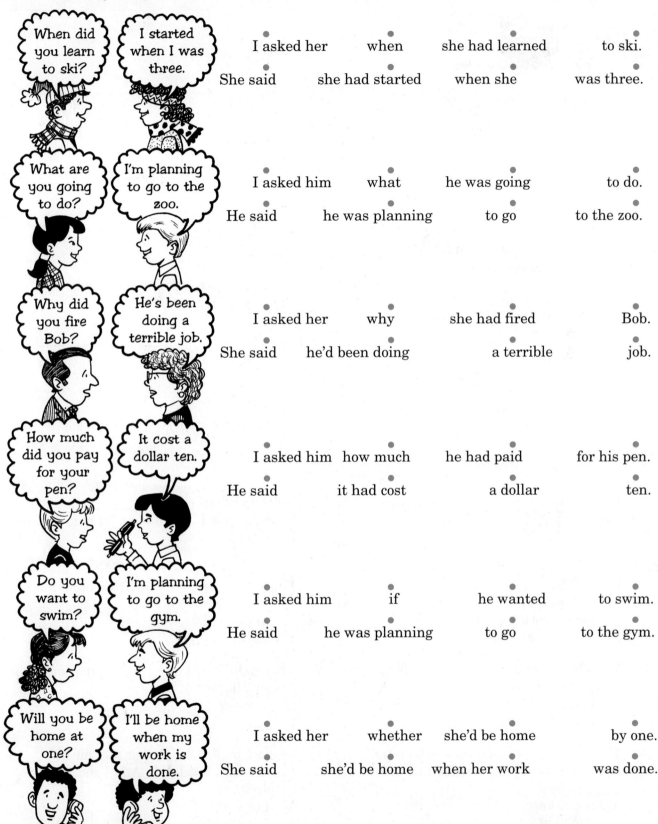

When did you learn to ski?

I started when I was three.

I asked her   when   she had learned   to ski.
She said   she had started   when she   was three.

What are you going to do?

I'm planning to go to the zoo.

I asked him   what   he was going   to do.
He said   he was planning   to go   to the zoo.

Why did you fire Bob?

He's been doing a terrible job.

I asked her   why   she had fired   Bob.
She said   he'd been doing   a terrible   job.

How much did you pay for your pen?

It cost a dollar ten.

I asked him   how much   he had paid   for his pen.
He said   it had cost   a dollar   ten.

Do you want to swim?

I'm planning to go to the gym.

I asked him   if   he wanted   to swim.
He said   he was planning   to go   to the gym.

Will you be home at one?

I'll be home when my work is done.

I asked her   whether   she'd be home   by one.
She said   she'd be home   when her work   was done.

K WHAT DID THEY TELL YOU?

1. Speak confidently!

   My teacher told me _____ <u>to speak confidently</u> _____.

2. Don't drive too fast!

   My parents told me _____.

3. Work quickly!

   My boss told me _____.

4. Don't eat too much candy!

   My doctor told me _____.

5. Don't play loud music!

   My neighbors told me _____.

L WHAT'S THE ANSWER?

1. We're getting worried about our son. We told him _____ by 11:00 P.M.
   a. to be home
   b. be home

2. Howard looks exhausted. I told him _____ so hard.
   a. not to work
   b. don't work

3. My doctor told me _____ exercising every day.
   a. start
   b. to start

4. The food at this restaurant is terrible! Now I know why my friends told me _____ here.
   a. not to eat
   b. don't eat

5. My supervisor told me _____ the report over because I had made a lot of mistakes.
   a. do
   b. to do

6. I'm really upset. My girlfriend told me _____ her anymore.
   a. to not call
   b. not to call

7. The teacher told us _____ Chapter 5, but I read Chapter 4.
   a. to read
   b. read

8. I'm in trouble! My father told me _____ his new car, but I did. And I got into an accident!
   a. not to drive
   b. to not drive

M EVERYBODY ALWAYS TELLS HIM WHAT TO DO

I'm tired of being told what to do. All day yesterday everybody told me what to do.

1. **Hurry! Your breakfast is getting cold.**

As soon as I woke up, my mother told me ___to hurry___.

She said ___my breakfast was getting cold___.

2. **Don't forget your umbrella! It's going to rain later.**

At breakfast my father told me _____

_____.

He said _____.

3. **Don't walk so slowly! We'll be late for school.**

On the way to school, my friend Jimmy told me _____

_____.

He said _____.

4. **Be quiet! You're disturbing the class!**

At school, Ms. Johnson told me _____

_____.

She said _____.

5. ....

....

When we were walking home from school, the police

officer on the corner told me _____.

He said _____.

(continued)

6.

When I went to soccer practice, my coach told me

_____.

He said _____.

7.

At my music lesson, my violin teacher told me

_____.

She said _____.

8.

When I was helping my family wash the dinner dishes,

my mother told me _____.

She said _____.

9.

_____! You'll fail your math test if you don't study.

I was hoping to watch TV after dinner, but my older

brother told me _____.

He said _____

_____.

10.

You have to get up early for school.

I couldn't even choose my own bedtime. My parents

told me _____.

They said _____.

I can't wait until I grow up! Then I can tell everybody else what to do!

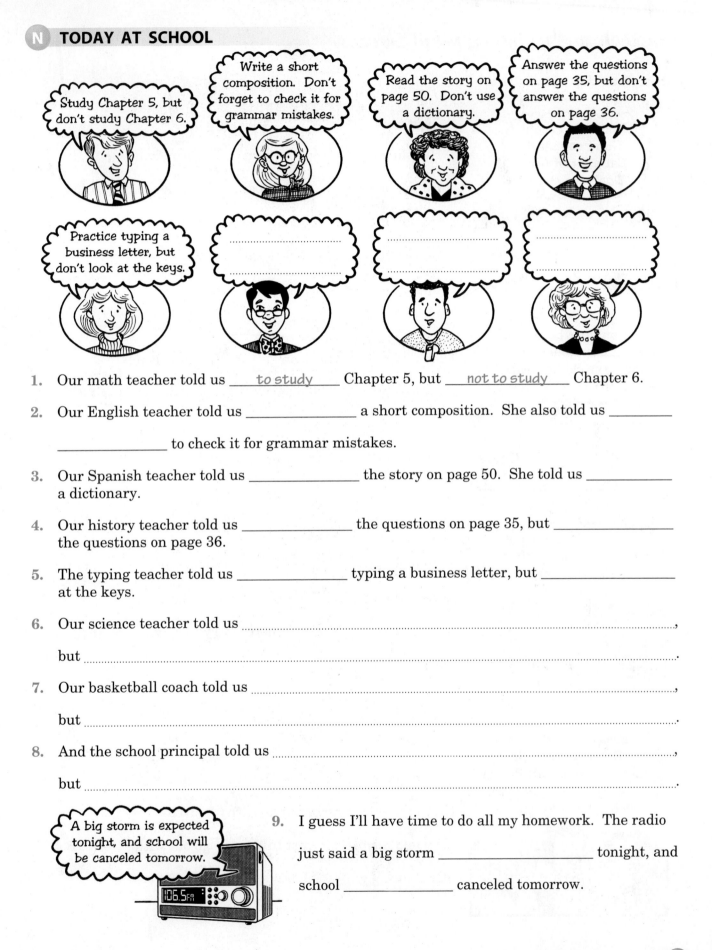

1. Our math teacher told us ___to study___ Chapter 5, but ___not to study___ Chapter 6.

2. Our English teacher told us _____ a short composition. She also told us _____

    _____ to check it for grammar mistakes.

3. Our Spanish teacher told us _____ the story on page 50. She told us _____
    a dictionary.

4. Our history teacher told us _____ the questions on page 35, but _____
    the questions on page 36.

5. The typing teacher told us _____ typing a business letter, but _____
    at the keys.

6. Our science teacher told us ....,

    but ....

7. Our basketball coach told us ....,

    but ....

8. And the school principal told us ....,

    but ....

9. I guess I'll have time to do all my homework. The radio

    just said a big storm _____ tonight, and

    school _____ canceled tomorrow.

Listen. Then clap and practice.

He told me · not to eat · candy.

He told me · not to eat · cake.

He told me · to eat · a lot of · fish.

He told me · not to eat · steak.

They told me · to clean · my bedroom.

They told me · to pick up · my toys.

They told me · to put · my clothes · away.

They told me · not to make · noise.

She told me · to come · to the meeting · at ten.

She told me · not to be · late.

She told me · to get there · early.

She told me · they wouldn't · wait.

They told me · to break up with · Harry.

They told me · to break up with · Ned.

They told me · not to · go out with · Bob

Or Barry · or Larry · or Fred.

P CHOOSE THE RIGHT WORD

1. Have you heard the news? A lion has (erased (escaped)) from the zoo!

2. This (calculator   casserole) tastes delicious! Who made it?

3. What's everybody so (talking   anxious) about?

4. Please remember to (lock   look) the door when you leave tonight.

5. My niece Nancy was the most beautiful (groom   bride) I've ever seen!

6. I think I'm getting the (flu   flew). I'd better call the doctor.

7. What can we do to (present   prevent) robberies in our neighborhood?

8. I'm sorry. I don't (no   know) how to do that, but I'll ask somebody.

9. This new (puddle   poodle) is the cutest puppy I've ever seen.

10. My landlord told me not to pour (pipes   grease) down the kitchen sink.

11. We felt very (reassured   rearranged) after we spoke to the police.

12. Did you know that the president wanted to raise (taxis   taxes)?

13. We can always depend on our parents to give us good (suggest   advice).

14. I'll be (away   way) from home all next week, but you can reach me by e-mail.

15. Did you hear that all the DVD players in the store are on (sail   sale) this week?

16. My parents asked me when I was going to (brake   break) up with my boyfriend.

17. I'm so excited! I just met a wonderful girl, and I think I'm (falling   failing) in love with her.

18. Somebody broke (out of   into) the house across the street and stole a lot of jewelry.

19. I'm a little (irritable   annoyed) at my neighbors. They're noisy, and they aren't very friendly.

20. The interviewer asked me why I thought I was (qualified   willing) for the position.

21. The teacher said we weren't allowed to use (examinations   dictionaries) during the test.

22. My friend Bill asked me (whether   weather) I wanted to go sailing, and I told him it was going to rain.

23. Michael and Sue got (engaged   married) last month, and they're going to get (engaged   married) in June.

Listen to each word and then say it.

st!	sk!	sp!
1. stand	9. skate	17. sports
2. start	10. ask	18. spring
3. fantastic	11. scare	19. special
4. rest	12. discover	20. hospital

ts!	ks!	ps!
5. that's	13. works	21. stops
6. patients	14. thinks	22. skips
7. writes	15. likes	23. helps
8. tickets	16. weeks	24. escapes

R   **WHO IS THE BEST?**

p   t   k   c

Fill in the missing letters and then read aloud.

Many pessimis _t_ s don't trus _t_ dentis _t_ s because they're s _c_ ared the wors__ will happen. However, Dr. Wes__'s patien__s are all optimis__ic. They think Dr. Wes__ is the bes__ dentis__ in Bos__on.

1. S__uart li__es Dr. Wes__.

Not only is he hones__, but he's the cheapes__ and the mos__ reliable dentis__ in Bos__on.

2. S__uar__'s sis__er also thin__s Dr. Wes__ is wonderful.

Dr. Wes__ wor__s very fas__ and never ma__es mis__a__es. He's the bes__ dentis__ on S__ate S__reet.

3. Mr. Jac__son can't s__and any other dentis__.

I go to Dr. Wes__ because I almos__ never feel any pain when I'm in his s__ecial dentis__'s chair. I could s__ay and res__ there all day.

4. Be__sy always tal__s about Dr. Wes__.

What I like mos__ about Dr. Wes__ is that he doesn't as__ a lot of questions when a patien__'s mouth is full of dental ins__rumen__s.

5. Dr. Wes__'s S__anish-s__eaking patien__s are es__ecially pleased.

Dr. Wes__ s__udies S__anish in his s__are time. We won't see any s__ecialis__ but Dr. Wes__.

6. Margaret is very enthusias__ic about Dr. Wes__.

One day I got the hiccu__s in his office. Dr. Wes__ jus__ s__opped and s__ood there waiting patiently. He didn't make me feel s__upid at all!

7. Patty thin__s Dr. Wes__ is the hardes__ working dentis__ she knows.

Dr. Wes__ never qui__s working all day. He even s__ips his lunch!

8. S__eve also li__es Dr. Wes__.

When I broke my leg playing bas__etball las__ s__ring, I missed two appointmen__s. Dr. Wes__ wasn't u__set at all. He even visited me in the hos__ital. We dis__ussed politi__s and s__orts. Tha__'s when I dis__overed that Dr. Wes__ li__es to s__i and s__ate.

A. Fill in the blanks.

1. George doesn't enjoy being a waiter. He wishes _____ an actor.

2. Ann took violin lessons last year and didn't enjoy them. She wishes _____ guitar lessons.

3. Frank drives an old used car. He wishes _____ a more reliable car.

4. By the time Jill got to the party, most of her friends had left. She wishes _____ to the party earlier.

5. I don't speak English very well. I wish _____ more fluently.

6. You ate all the ice cream in the refrigerator! I wish _____ it all!

B. Complete the sentences.

1. The Johnsons didn't enjoy their vacation because the weather wasn't warm.

    If the weather _____ warm, they _____ their vacation.

2. My doctor is concerned because I eat too many rich desserts.

    If I _____ so many rich desserts, my doctor _____ concerned.

3. Gloria arrived late because she missed the bus.

    If she _____ the bus, _____ late.

4. I'm frustrated because I can't type very fast.

    If _____ fast, _____ so frustrated.

5. You made a lot of mistakes because you weren't paying attention.

    If you _____ attention, you _____ so many mistakes.

6. Gary looks confused because he doesn't understand today's grammar.

    If he _____ today's grammar, he _____ so confused.

C. Complete the sentences.

Ex. I'm feeling fine after my operation.

    Uncle Bill called. He said he ____was feeling____ fine after his operation.

1. *I got a big promotion.*

    My friend Betty called. She said _____ a big promotion.

2. *What's your name?*

   The police officer asked me _____.

3. *Did you see me on TV last night?*

   My friend Rita called. She asked me _____ on TV last night.

4. *I'm sorry I forgot your birthday.*

   My sister-in-law called. She said _____ my birthday.

5. *I won't be able to visit you this weekend.*

   Grandpa called. He said _____ us this weekend.

6. *Brush your teeth every day, and don't eat any candy.*

   My dentist told me _____ my teeth every day, and _____
   any candy.

7. *When will I be old enough to drive?*

   My son asked me _____ old enough to drive.

8. *Why are you leaving so early? Are you in a hurry to get somewhere?*

   Aunt Martha asked me _____ so early. She wanted to know

   _____ to get somewhere.

D. Listening 🔊

Listen and complete the sentences.

Ex. (a.) I'd be able to see a movie.
    b. I had seen a movie.

1. a. I wouldn't have had to stay home in bed.
    b. I had to stay in bed.

2. a. I hadn't gotten depressed so often.
    b. I wouldn't get depressed so often.

3. a. we had forgotten to pay our rent.
    b. he'll call us back tonight.

4. a. when are we going to get married.
    b. when we were going to get married.

5. a. if I had gone to college.
    b. whether had I gone to college.

Read the article on student book page 125 and answer the questions.

STUDENT BOOK PAGES 125–128

1. The most important tip for a successful interview is to _____.
   a. be prepared
   b. brag about yourself
   c. write a thank-you note
   d. fill out an application

2. A good way to find out about a company is to _____.
   a. read job ads
   b. ask the interviewer
   c. look up the address
   d. use the Internet

3. During the interview, you should _____.
   a. tell about your family
   b. answer questions honestly
   c. ask about benefits
   d. ask about vacations

4. In paragraph 2, *dress appropriately* means _____.
   a. stand out from the crowd
   b. wear casual clothes
   c. dress neatly and in nice clothes
   d. dress in comfortable clothes

5. The interviewer will probably NOT ask about your _____.
   a. age
   b. education
   c. strengths
   d. plans for the future

6. You can expect an interviewer to _____.
   a. arrive late
   b. tell you about his or her background
   c. ask about your weaknesses
   d. ask you to come to a follow-up interview

7. *Get along with* in paragraph 3 means _____.
   a. supervise
   b. give instructions to
   c. do the same job as
   d. be friendly with

8. You can infer from the article that an interview _____.
   a. will probably last for an hour
   b. is an important way that companies evaluate job applicants
   c. is easy if you've never had one
   d. isn't challenging for most people

B POINTS IN A TEXT: Identifying Examples that Support the Author's Points

In the article about interview skills, the author makes points about good interview skills and gives examples to explain and support these points. Match the points and examples in the article.

_____ 1. Learn about the company before the interview.

_____ 2. Prepare for the questions you will be asked.

_____ 3. Dress appropriately for the interview.

_____ 4. Prepare questions to ask the interviewer.

_____ 5. Follow up after the interview.

a. Don't wear casual clothes.
b. Be ready to explain why you want to leave your current job.
c. Write a thank-you letter to the interviewer.
d. Look at the company's website for information.
e. Ask about the job responsibilities.

C FACT FILE

Look at the Fact File on student book page 125 and answer the questions.

1. The second most common way to find a job is to _____.
   a. network
   b. go to an employment agency
   c. read the want ads
   d. write to or call the company yourself

2. More than one-third (1/3) of job applicants find their jobs by _____.
   a. reading the newspaper
   b. contacting an employer directly
   c. communicating with other people
   d. using an employment agency

D WHO GOT THE JOB?

Read the article on student book page 126 and answer the questions.

1. When asked about her experience, Sarah Jones _____.
   a. only talked about her education
   b. talked about her family
   c. gave a lot of information
   d. asked about the company

2. Sarah wants to leave her current job because _____.
   a. it isn't challenging enough
   b. it's too challenging
   c. she wants to travel more
   d. she has a lot of weaknesses

3. Sarah thinks she needs to _____ better.
   a. use computer software
   b. ask questions at an interview
   c. write follow-up notes
   d. write business letters

4. Bob wasn't familiar with the company's products because _____.
   a. he didn't need any software
   b. he hadn't prepared for the interview
   c. the interviewer didn't tell him
   d. he didn't have Internet access

5. Sarah made a better impression because _____.
   a. she asked about vacation days
   b. she wanted to work shorter hours
   c. she knew about the company
   d. she hadn't thought about her weaknesses

6. You can infer that Bob's interview _____.
   a. was longer than Sarah's
   b. was cancelled by the interviewer
   c. was successful
   d. was shorter than Sarah's

E AROUND THE WORLD

Read the article on student book page 126 and answer the questions.

1. In the U.S., interviewers do NOT usually ask about _____.
   a. language skills
   b. marital status
   c. educational background
   d. future plans

2. Eye contact is an example of _____.
   a. body language
   b. formality
   c. rudeness
   d. personality

3. A firm handshake is unusual in _____.
   a. Mexico
   b. Germany
   c. France
   d. the U.S.

4. The main idea of the article is that interviews _____ around the world.
   a. are similar
   b. are informal
   c. are formal
   d. are different

F INTERVIEW

Read the interview on student book page 127 and answer the questions.

1. Monica Salinas interviews _____.
   a. about 10 people a week
   b. about 50 people a day
   c. about 50 people a week
   d. about 100 people a year

2. She asks applicants about weekend activities because _____.
   a. she learns about applicants this way
   b. she's interested in hobbies
   c. they need to work weekends
   d. she's a friendly person

3. One applicant ate his sandwich during the interview because _____.
   a. he was nervous
   b. he was confident
   c. he wasn't prepared
   d. he was hungry

4. An employee from Brazil received a bonus check because _____.
   a. she sent money to her family
   b. she was a hard worker
   c. she was promoted
   d. she was given a raise

5. According to Monica Salinas, the best advice for interviews is to _____.
   a. reschedule them
   b. talk only about yourself
   c. be serious and honest
   d. be relaxed and be yourself

6. You can infer that Monica Salinas _____.
   a. works overtime
   b. will be promoted
   c. enjoys her job
   d. works in an international company

G YOU'RE THE INTERVIEWER!

Imagine you're a Human Resources manager. Interview a classmate for a job at your company. Write the answers below. Then role-play the interview for the class.

Tell me about your background and experience.	
How would a friend describe you? (Suggest at least four words that person might use.)	
What do you enjoy doing on the weekend? Do you have any hobbies?	
What would you be able to contribute to our company?	

H FUN WITH IDIOMS

Choose the best response.

1. Aunt Dorothy talks my head off.
   a. Did you call her back?
   b. I know. She never says much.
   c. Yes. She's a good speaker.
   d. It's true. She's never quiet.

2. Frank really put his foot in his mouth.
   a. I was surprised it fit.
   b. I think he should apologize.
   c. He was very prepared.
   d. It was a nice thing for him to say.

3. Our boss never beats around the bush.
   a. Yes. She always says what she's thinking.
   b. Is she a gardener?
   c. That can be confusing.
   d. Is it difficult to understand her?

4. I think Richard inflated his resume.
   a. That was a good idea.
   b. It's good to have a long resume.
   c. He should have been honest.
   d. I know. It's very short.

WE'VE GOT MAIL!

Choose the words that best complete each sentence.

1. Marcy said she wouldn't be able to come to the party. She said she _____ sorry.
   - a. is being
   - b. had been
   - c. will be
   - d. was

2. We heard from Uncle Carl. He said he _____ visiting us this spring.
   - a. has been
   - b. can be
   - c. wouldn't be
   - d. had been

3. The tenants told the owner of the building they _____ upset with the superintendent.
   - a. been
   - b. were
   - c. will be
   - d. have been being

Choose the sentence that is correct and complete.

7. a. She told me she was surprised.
   b. She told me she has surprised.
   c. She told me she had surprised.
   d. She told me she being surprised.

8. a. He said he hasn't going to be late.
   b. He said he wasn't going to be late.
   c. He said he hadn't going to be late.
   d. He said he not going to be late.

9. a. I knew that the Nile be in Egypt.
   b. I knew that the Nile being in Egypt.
   c. I knew that the Nile is in Egypt.
   d. I knew that the Nile been in Egypt.

4. All the students in our class knew that Sacramento _____ the capital of California.
   - a. is
   - b. being
   - c. be
   - d. been

5. They asked me where yesterday's meeting _____ held.
   - a. is
   - b. has been
   - c. had
   - d. had been

6. Our teacher told us that making eye contact _____ considered rude.
   - a. hasn't
   - b. isn't
   - c. being
   - d. hasn't been being

10. a. He asked me where the bank be.
    b. He asked me where the bank was.
    c. He asked me where the bank being.
    d. He asked me where the bank been.

11. a. Nobody knew where she is.
    b. Nobody knew where she be.
    c. Nobody knew where she been.
    d. Nobody knew where she had been.

12. a. They said they could help us.
    b. They said they can help us.
    c. They said they helping us.
    d. They said they be helping us.

"CAN-DO" REVIEW

Match the "can do" statement and the correct sentence.

_____ 1. I can express certainty.

_____ 2. I can express agreement.

_____ 3. I can ask for a reason.

_____ 4. I can make a deduction.

_____ 5. I can empathize.

_____ 6. I can express a wish about something in the present.

_____ 7. I can express a wish about something in the past.

_____ 8. I can report what people have said.

_____ 9. I can express surprise.

_____ 10. I can express feelings and emotions.

a. Why do you say that?

b. I can't believe it!

c. I know what you mean.

d. I wish I had studied more for yesterday's test.

e. I suppose you're right.

f. He said he wouldn't be able to come to work.

g. We're annoyed at our landlord.

h. I'm positive.

i. I wish we lived in a larger apartment.

j. He must have been driving too fast.

A WHAT ARE THEY SAYING?

1. Mrs. Webber will be back soon, _____won't she_____?

2. I can park here, _____?

3. You live around the corner, _____?

4. You brought the plane tickets, _____?

5. I'm going to play today, _____?

6. We've hiked far enough, _____?

7. Santa Claus will be here soon, _____?

8. You were once a Broadway star, _____?

9. This is supposed to be a person, _____?

10. You're still in love with me, _____?

WHAT'S THE TAG?

1. The computer is working, _____?
   a. isn't it
   b. doesn't it

2. We've eaten here before, _____?
   a. haven't we
   b. didn't we

3. I'm on time, _____?
   a. amn't I
   b. aren't I

4. He'll be in the office next week, _____?
   a. won't he
   b. isn't he

5. You finished your report, _____?
   a. don't you
   b. didn't you

6. They're going to leave soon, _____?
   a. won't they
   b. aren't they

7. She was at the meeting, _____?
   a. wasn't she
   b. isn't she

8. Timmy, this baby food tastes good, _____?
   a. isn't it
   b. doesn't it

C I THINK I KNOW YOU

A. Excuse me, but I think I know you. You're a student

   at City College, _____ aren't you _____¹?

B. Yes, _____².

A. That's what I thought. I was sure I had seen you there, but I've forgotten when. Now I remember! You've been

   in a lot of school plays, _____³?

B. Yes, _____⁴.

A. That's what I thought. And you sang in the school chorus last year, _____⁵?

B. Yes, as a matter of fact, _____⁶.

A. I thought so. And now that I think of it, I've also seen you on Winter Street. You live there,

   _____⁷?

B. Yes, _____⁸.

A. Isn't this ridiculous? I can remember so much about you, but I still can't remember your name.

   Wait . . . Now I remember. Your name is Mandy, _____⁹?

B. No, it _____¹⁰.

A. It isn't?! I was sure your name was Mandy.

B. That's what everybody thinks. I'm Sandy. Mandy is my twin sister.

D WHAT ARE THEY SAYING?

1. The post office hasn't closed yet, __has it__?

2. You aren't allergic to nuts, _____?

3. You don't still go out with Larry, _____?

4. I didn't hit you, _____?

5. I'm not permitted to skateboard here, _____?

6. You won't forget to call, _____?

7. We haven't run out of milk, _____?

8. This apartment doesn't have cockroaches, _____?

9. Yesterday wasn't our anniversary, _____?

10. Today isn't your birthday, _____?

D **126** Activity Workbook

When I woke up yesterday morning, I knew right away it was going to be a terrible day. I knew that everything was going to go wrong all day and that I couldn't do ANYTHING about it. My problems started the minute I got up.

1. Breakfast isn't ready yet, _____is it____?

No, ___it isn't___.

That's what I thought.

2. I don't have time to take a shower, _____?

No, _____.

That's what I thought.

3. I lost my English book. You haven't seen it anywhere, _____?

No, _____.

That's what I thought.

4. There isn't any more orange juice, _____?

No, _____.

That's what I thought.

5. My shirt hasn't been ironed yet, _____?

No, _____.

That's what I thought.

6. I won't be able to finish my breakfast, _____?

No, _____.

That's what I thought.

I arrived an hour late for school. My problems continued there.

7. School didn't start late today, _____?

No, _____.

That's what I thought.

8. The teachers aren't all home sick today, _____?

No, _____.

That's what I thought.

(continued)

9. Today's math test wasn't canceled, _____?

No, _____.

That's what I thought.

10. I can't hand in today's history assignment next week, _____?

No, _____.

That's what I thought.

11. They aren't serving anything except "Tuna Surprise" casserole for lunch today, _____?

No, _____.

That's what I thought.

F WHAT'S THE TAG?

1. They aren't having problems, _____?
   a. are they
   b. aren't they

2. George was hired, _____?
   a. was he
   b. wasn't he

3. You didn't have to work overtime, _____?
   a. did you
   b. didn't you

4. You've done your homework, _____?
   a. have you
   b. haven't you

5. I'm not late, _____?
   a. aren't I
   b. am I

6. The bank will be open tomorrow, _____?
   a. will it
   b. won't it

7. He wants to marry you, _____?
   a. doesn't he
   b. is he

8. Your mother isn't upset, _____?
   a. isn't she
   b. is she

9. I can skate on this pond, _____?
   a. can I
   b. can't I

10. You received my letter, _____?
    a. didn't you
    b. did you

11. There wasn't a big storm, _____?
    a. was there
    b. wasn't there

12. I'm going to be promoted, _____?
    a. am I
    b. aren't I

13. Your son has been here before, _____?
    a. hasn't he
    b. has he

14. You won't be upset if I'm late, _____?
    a. won't you
    b. will you

Listen and complete the sentences.

1. a. do you?
   b.⃝ don't you?

2. a. aren't you?
   b. are you?

3. a. do we?
   b. don't we?

4. a. did you?
   b. didn't you?

5. a. does she?
   b. doesn't he?

6. a. haven't you?
   b. have you?

7. a. was she?
   b. wasn't she?

8. a. hasn't he?
   b. has he?

9. a. won't we?
   b. will we?

10. a. can we?
    b. can't we?

11. a. is it?
    b. isn't it?

12. a. didn't I?
    b. did I?

H **YOU DECIDE:** *A Good Father*

I can't understand why I've been having so many problems with my son, Timmy. After all,

I'm a good father, _____aren't I_____ ¹? I usually try to be patient, _____²?

I'm not very strict, _____³? And I'm always nice to his friends, _____⁴?

Also, I've always _____⁵, _____⁶?

I didn't _____⁷, _____⁸?

When he was little, I _____⁹, _____¹⁰?

And now that he's older, I _____¹¹, _____¹²?

I'm not _____¹³, _____¹⁴?

I don't _____¹⁵, _____¹⁶?

And I'm always there when he needs me, _____¹⁷? So what could have gone
wrong?

I GRAMMARRAP: *She Drives to Work, Doesn't She?*

Listen. Then clap and practice.

She drives   to work,   doesn't she?

She was   late,   wasn't she?

He doesn't   type well,   does he?

He wasn't   hired,   was he?

I work   very hard,   don't I?

I'll get   a raise,   won't I?

I shouldn't   buy it,   should I?

I wouldn't be   sorry,   would I?

You know them   well,   don't you?

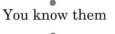

You'll intro   duce me,   won't you?

We should   see it,   shouldn't we?

We'd   enjoy it,   wouldn't we?

You love to   dance,   don't you?

You'll come to   the party,   won't you?

SURPRISES

1. A. You haven't been standing in the rain long, ___have you___?

   B. I'm afraid ___I have___.

   A. ___You have___?! I'm really sorry. I had no idea it was so late.

2. A. Barbara is going to law school next year, _____?

   B. No, _____.

   A. _____?! I thought she wanted to be a lawyer like her mother.

3. A. Alan won't be graduating from college this year, _____?

   B. Yes, _____.

   A. _____?! I can't believe the time has gone by so fast.

4. A. Our spring vacation begins tomorrow, _____?

   B. No, _____.

   A. _____?! I'm really surprised. I've been looking forward to tomorrow all month.

5. A. It's time to eat. You brought the sandwiches, _____?

   B. Sandwiches?! No, _____.

   A. _____?! How could you have forgotten? I was sure you were going to bring them.

6. A. Ricky doesn't drive yet, _____?

   B. I know it's hard to believe, but _____.

   A. _____?! I can remember when he was just learning how to walk. Children grow up so quickly.

K WHAT ARE THEY SAYING?

1. A. You were expecting us, ___weren't you___?
   B. Actually, I wasn't.
   A. You weren't?! I'm really surprised! I was

   sure ___you had been expecting___ us.

2. A. You have medical insurance, _____?
   B. Actually, I don't.
   A. You don't?! That's very surprising! I was

   sure _____ medical insurance.

3. A. She's been here before, _____?
   B. Actually, she hasn't.
   A. She hasn't?! I'm surprised! I was sure

   _____ here before.

4. A. He isn't going to be transferred, _____?
   B. Actually, he is.
   A. He is?! I don't believe it! I was sure

   _____ transferred.

5. A. We can leave early today, _____?
   B. Actually, we can't.
   A. We can't?! I'm really surprised! I

   was sure _____ early.

6. A. This suit is on sale, _____?
   B. Actually, it isn't.
   A. It isn't?! I can't believe it! I was

   sure this suit _____ on sale.

7. A. I don't have to work overtime, _____?
   B. Actually, you do.
   A. I do?! I can't believe it! I was sure

   _____ have to work overtime.

8. A. You'll marry her someday, _____?
   B. Actually, I won't.
   A. You won't?! I'm surprised! I was sure

   _____ her someday.

L LISTENING

Listen and complete the conversations.

1. a. she had been a doctor.
   b. she was going to be a doctor.

2. a. you had sold your house.
   b. you didn't sell your house.

3. a. it had new brakes.
   b. it has new brakes.

4. a. you aren't angry with me.
   b. you weren't angry with me.

5. a. they would be arriving this weekend.
   b. they'll be arriving this weekend.

6. a. you got searched.
   b. you hadn't gotten searched.

7. a. children were allowed to see it.
   b. children weren't allowed to see it.

8. a. he still worked at the bank.
   b. he still works at the bank.

9. a. she had been hired by the Bay Company.
   b. she was hired by the Bay Company.

10. a. he can deliver babies.
    b. he could deliver babies.

Central High School Reunion

1. A. Do you ever see our old friend Susan? She was one of the nicest people in our class.

   B. As a matter of fact, I see her all the time. I married her!

   A. _____You did_____?! I don't believe it! You ____didn't____

   really ____marry____ Susan, ____did you____?

   B. Yes, ____I did____.

2. A. Do you still go canoeing every weekend?

   B. Not anymore. I'm MUCH too busy. I have three small children at home.

   A. _____?! I never would have believed it!

   You _____ really _____ three children,

   _____?

   B. Yes, _____.

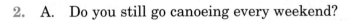

3. A. Do you still work for an insurance company?

   B. Not anymore. As a matter of fact, I'm the president of my own company.

   A. _____?! I don't believe it! You _____

   really the president of your own company,

   _____?

   B. Yes, _____.

4. A. Do you keep in touch with Julie Montero?

   B. Yes. I see her all the time. As a matter of fact, she was just chosen "Employee of the Year" at her company.

   A. _____?! That's fantastic! She _____

   really _____ "Employee of the Year," _____?

   B. Yes, _____.

(continued)

5.   A.   I wonder whatever happened to Margaret Wong.

      B.   Well, the last time I saw her she had just won a million dollars on a TV game show.

      A.   _____?! That's unbelievable! She _____

          really _____ a million dollars, _____?

      B.   Yes, _____.

6.   A.   Have you heard? Vincent Lewis quit his job and

          ....

      B.   _____?! I can't believe it! He _____

          really do that, _____?

      A.   Yes, _____.

7.   A.   Tell me about your son, Billy. I hear he's a very special little boy.

      B.   You don't really want to hear about Billy, _____?

      A.   Yes, of course. I'm very interested.

      B.   Well, Billy is only four years old, but he can ....

          ....

          and ....

      A.   _____?! I don't believe it! He _____

          really do all those things, _____?

      B.   Yes, _____.

8.   A.   How's little Patty?

      B.   My daughter Patty isn't so little anymore. She's going to

          .... next month.

      A.   _____?! I don't believe it! She _____ really

          going to _____ next month, _____?
          She was just a baby the last time I saw her.

1. A. You know . . . you've been a little "touchy" recently.

   B. I guess you're right. I ___have___ been a little "touchy" recently, ___haven't I___!

2. A. You know, we shouldn't be fishing here.

   B. I suppose you're right. We _____ be fishing here, _____!

3. A. I think our guests had a great time at our party.

   B. I agree. They _____ a great time, _____!

4. A. You know . . . the people in this neighborhood aren't very friendly.

   B. You're right. They _____ very friendly, _____!

5. A. Mr. Mudge is in a terrible mood today.

   B. I agree. He _____ in a terrible mood today, _____!

6. A. You know . . . this pizza tastes terrible!

   B. You're right. This pizza _____ terrible, _____!

7. A. You know, I hate to say it, but you were impolite to the boss.

   B. I guess you're right. I _____ impolite to the boss, _____!

8. A. You know . . . I think we'll have to work overtime this weekend.

   B. I'm afraid you're right. We _____ have to work overtime, _____!

9. A. You know . . . we haven't called Grandma in a long time.

   B. You're right. We _____ called her in a long time, _____!

10. A. I'm sorry to say it, but that tie looks terrible with that shirt!

    B. I guess you're right. It _____ terrible with this shirt, _____!

11. You know . . . you drove through that intersection too fast!

    You're right. I _____ through that intersection too fast, _____!

A. I'm thinking of breaking up with my boyfriend, Howard.

B. I don't believe it. Why do you want to break up with Howard? He's a wonderful person. He's kind and generous.

A. I guess he ___is___¹ kind and generous, ___isn't he___²!

B. And he sends you flowers all the time.

A. Come to think of it, he _____³ _____⁴ me flowers all the time, _____⁵!

B. And he's _____⁶.

A. I guess you're right. He _____⁷, _____⁸!

B. And remember last month. Howard gave you _____⁹, and you were very happy.

A. Come to think of it, he _____¹⁰ _____¹¹ me _____¹²

last month, _____¹³! And I _____¹⁴ very happy, _____¹⁵!

B. Yes. But I really wasn't surprised because he's always given you a lot of presents.

A. That's true. He _____¹⁶ always _____¹⁷ me a lot of presents, _____¹⁸!

B. Here's something else to think about. He doesn't _____¹⁹.

A. You're right. He _____²⁰, _____²¹!

B. Also, _____²².

A. Come to think of it, that's true. _____²³,

_____²⁴!

B. And how do you think Howard would feel? He'd be very upset if you broke up with him.

A. I'm afraid you're right. He _____²⁵ be very upset, _____²⁶! You know, I'm glad I talked to you. I guess I won't break up with Howard after all.

LISTENING

Listen to each word and then say it.

1. <u>b</u>oat
2. <u>b</u>etter
3. a<u>b</u>out
4. <u>b</u>ought
5. <u>b</u>right

6. <u>v</u>ote
7. <u>v</u>acation
8. a<u>v</u>oid
9. o<u>v</u>en
10. tra<u>v</u>el

11. <u>w</u>on't
12. <u>w</u>eather
13. a<u>w</u>ay
14. <u>w</u>indow
15. <u>w</u>orry

Q B<u>E</u>VERLY <u>W</u>ILSON'S <u>B</u>ROKEN KEY<u>B</u>OARD

Beverly Wilson's keyboard is broken. The b's, v's, and w's don't always work. Fill in the missing b's, v's, and w's, and then read Beverly's letters aloud.

1.

Dear <u>B</u>etty,

You'<u>v</u>e pro__a__ly heard from Bo__ a__out the terri__le ro____eries __e'__e __een ha__ing in our neighborhood. (There ha__e __een se__en ro____eries in fi__e __eeks!) Of course, e__ery__ody's __een __ery __orried __ecause they still ha__en't disco__ered who the ro____ers are.

Last __ednesday, my neigh__or's __icycle __as stolen from his __asement. The next e__ening, some__ody __roke into a __uilding on __righton __oule__ard and took se__eral sil__er __racelets, a __allet, and t__o __edding rings.

Then last __eekend, __elie__e it or not, the Relia__le __ank __as ro____ed. I'll al__ays remem__er the e__ening of the ro____ery. I __as taking a __ath, and my hus__and, __ill, __as reading his fa__orite no__el in __ed __hen Ro__er __egan __arking. He must ha__e heard the ro____ers dri__ing a__ay. __y the time I got out of the __athtu__, e__ery__ody in the neigh__orhood __as talking a__out the ro____ers' escape.

__ell, e__er since the __ank ro____ery last __eekend, __e'__e all __een __ery ner__ous. Some of the neigh__ors are so __orried that they're thinking a__out mo__ing a__ay. __ill and I ha__e __een __ondering __hat __e should do.

Lo__e,

__e__erly

(continued)

2.

Dear __etsy,

 __e're ha__ing a __edding anni__ersary cele__ration on __ednesday for my __rother-in-law, __arry, and his wife, Ro__erta, and __e __ould lo__e it if you and your hus__and, __alter, __ere there. It __on't __e a __ery __ig cele__ration, just a few relati__es, __illiam, __incent, Eliza__eth, Ste__e, and of course my __rothers and their __i__es.

 __e've heard that your __rother's little __oy __o___y is __isiting you this __eek. __hy don't you __ring him along __ith you __hen you come o__er on __ednesday?

Lo__e,

__e__erly

3.

Dear Al__ert,

 __e're ha__ing a __onderful time on our __acation in __oston, __ut __e __ish you and your __ife __ere here __ith us. I'm positi__e __oth you and __ar__ara __ould lo__e it here. __ar__ara __ould lo__e the __oston Pu__lic Garden and the __oats on the Charles Ri__er. And you __ould ha__e a __onderful time __isiting the uni__ersities and the __oston Pu__lic Li__rary. __e're staying __ith __ill's relati__es __hile __e're in __oston. They li__e in a __ery modern high-rise __uilding __ith a __eautiful __iew of the ri__er. __e'__e __een __ery lucky. __ill's relati__es dri__e us e__ery__here.

 The __eather in __oston __as __ery __arm __hen __e arri__ed, but now it's __indy. I __ish __e had __rought __armer clothes to __ear.

 __y the __ay, __ill and I __ent to a li__ely __ase__all game last __ednesday, and __e'__e __een to the __allet t__ice. __e'__e also __een __ery __usy __uying presents for e__ery__ody at home and sou__enirs for oursel__es. (Unfortunately, __e __eren't a__le to __uy the __atch your __rother __alter __anted.)

Lo__e,

__e__erly

1. I don't feel like _____.
    a. take a walk
    (b.) taking a walk

2. I never get tired _____.
    a. of going on picnics
    b. to go on picnics

3. I'm not going to work out today. _____
    at the gym yesterday.
    a. If I had worked out
    b. I worked out

4. My friends and I usually love _____
    the mall.
    a. going to
    b. going

5. Thanks. _____ to have dinner with you.
    a. I'll like
    b. I'd like

6. _____ go sailing?
    a. Would you like
    b. Would you like to

7. I'd be happy _____ you to the airport.
    a. to take
    b. take

8. _____ a movie yesterday, I'd be happy
    to go with you today.
    a. If I hadn't seen
    b. If I saw

9. I won't be able to go to your son's
    wedding. I hope _____.
    a. you understand
    b. I understand

10. _____ you can't go bowling with us.
    a. I'd be disappointed
    b. I'm disappointed

B WHAT ARE THEY SAYING?

1. I really don't feel like ___eating___
    at a restaurant with my friends tonight.

    I _____ at a restaurant last night.

2. Do you think _____ get tired of

    _____ dancing if you

    _____ dancing all the time?

3. I don't feel like _____ TV today.

    If I _____ TV all day

    yesterday, _____ certainly watch it
    today.

4. I've _____ the dishes every day
    this week, and I'm really tired of

    _____ them. I'd be happy

    _____ the dishes some other
    time, but not tonight!

WHAT ARE THEY SAYING?

see

A. Do you really want _____to see____ ¹ a movie again tonight?   I know

you enjoy _____ ² movies, but you've already

_____ ³ four movies this week, and you just

_____ ⁴ a movie this afternoon.   Don't you EVER get

tired of _____ ⁵ movies?   If I were you, I

certainly _____ ⁶ another movie tonight.

B. Maybe I'm a little crazy, but there's nothing I like more than

_____ ⁷ movies.   I really DO feel like _____ ⁸

a movie with you tonight, and believe it or not, I'm planning

_____ ⁹ another movie tomorrow!

go

A. We're _____ ¹⁰ camping this weekend.   Would you

like to come with us?

B. I don't really feel like _____ ¹¹ camping this

weekend.   To be honest, I don't enjoy _____ ¹² camping.

A. You don't?!   I thought you _____ ¹³ camping all the time!

B. I do, but that's only because everybody else in my family loves

_____ ¹⁴ camping.   If you really want to know the

truth, I can't stand _____ ¹⁵ camping!   Ever since I

first _____ ¹⁶ camping years ago, I've hated it!   If my

family didn't enjoy _____ ¹⁷ camping so much,

I'd never _____ ¹⁸ camping at all!

A. I'm sorry you feel that way.   I'll never ask you _____ ¹⁹ camping

again!

GRAMMARRAP: *I Suppose You'd Get Tired*

Listen. Then clap and practice.

I suppose you'd   get tired of   driving   downtown
If you drove   downtown   every day.
You would also   get tired of   driving   around
If you didn't   know   your way.

I suppose you'd   get tired of   eating   cheese
If you ate it   at every   meal.
You'd probably   get   a bad stomachache
And complain about   how   you feel.

I suppose you'd   get tired of   typing   reports
If you typed them   without   taking breaks.
If you didn't   stop   and rest   for a while,
Your reports would be   full of   mistakes.

I suppose   I'd get tired of   having   cake
If I had some   each night   for dinner.
If I had   more fruit   instead of   cake
I'd probably   be   a lot thinner.

I suppose you'd   get tired of   watching   TV
If you always   watched the same shows.
If you listened to   music   or read   a book,
You wouldn't   be bored,   I suppose.

E THEY NEVER WOULD HAVE DONE THAT!

1. Emily hit the wrong key and deleted all her files.

   If _____she hadn't hit_____ the wrong key,

   she never ___would have deleted___ all her files.

2. Henry drove into a tree because he was daydreaming.

   If _____ daydreaming, he never

   _____ into a tree.

3. I got a terrible score on my SAT because during the test I had my mind on something else.

   If _____ my mind on something else,

   I never _____ a terrible score.

4. My wife and I were an hour late to the party because we misunderstood the directions.

   If _____ the directions,

   we never _____ an hour late to the party.

5. Albert decided to take a bath, and he forgot to take his cake out of the oven.

   If _____ to take a bath,

   he never _____ to take his cake out of the oven.

6. Alice put salt in her coffee. She thought it was sugar.

   If _____ it was sugar,

   she never _____ salt in her coffee.

7. Mr. and Mrs. Jackson accidentally mixed up their video tapes, and they erased the video of their wedding.

   If _____ their video tapes,

   they never _____ the video of their wedding.

Listen. Then clap and practice.

I'm very   sorry   I took   your CD.

I must have   thought   it belonged   to me.

I'm sorry   it's midnight,   and now   you're awake.

I must have   called you   by   mistake.

The cake was   bad,   and it's all   my fault.

I must have   mixed up   the sugar   and salt.

I'm sorry   I shouted.   I know   I was rude.

I must have   been   in a very bad   mood.

G **YOU DECIDE:** *I'm Really Sorry*

1. You've been invited to a party. You arrive on the wrong day. Your friends are cleaning their house!

YOUR FRIENDS: What a nice surprise! As you can see, we're getting ready for tomorrow's party.

YOU: ....

YOUR FRIENDS: ....

YOU: ....

2. You've been stopped by a police officer because you went through a red light at the last intersection.

POLICE OFFICER: You just drove through a red light! Didn't you see it?

YOU: ....

POLICE OFFICER: ....

YOU: ....

WHAT ARE THEY SAYING?

1. A. My husband is out of work.

    B. What a shame! How long

    ____has he been____ out of work?

    A. ____For____ more than two months.

3. A. I'm having trouble concentrating
        on my work.

    B. That's too bad. How long _____

    _____

    concentrating on your work?

    A. _____ I moved to Hawaii.

5. A. My knees hurt!

    B. I'm sorry to hear that. How long

    _____?

    A. _____ the past few weeks.

7. A. My employees are on strike.

    B. They are? How long _____

    _____ on strike?

    A. _____ more than a month.

2. A. My house has termites!

    B. That's terrible! How long _____

    _____ termites?

    A. _____ last summer.

4. A. I've been feeling a little depressed
        recently.

    B. That's a shame How long _____

    _____ depressed?

    A. _____ my girlfriend broke up
    with me.

6. A. My car is at the repair shop.

    B. Oh, really? How long _____

    _____ at the repair shop?

    A. _____ last Monday.

8. A. My wife wants to buy a motorcycle.

    B. She does?! How long _____

    _____ a motorcycle?

    A. _____ her fortieth birthday.

WHAT'S WRONG?

for	since

DOCTOR: How long have you been sick, Mr. Lawson?

PATIENT: I've been sick _____ _since_ ¹ last Tuesday.

DOCTOR: I see. How long have you had a pain in your chest?

PATIENT: I've had a pain in my chest _____ ² about three days.

And I've had a backache _____ ³ last week.

DOCTOR: You have a fever, too. Do you know how long you've had a fever?

PATIENT: _____ ⁴ the past week. Also, I've felt dizzy _____ ⁵ I got the fever.

DOCTOR: Tell me, Mr. Lawson, have you been working?

PATIENT: No, I've been at home _____ ⁶ April 2nd. And I've been in bed _____ ⁷ about a week. I've been very tired.

I've been sleeping _____ ⁸ about 14 hours a day.

DOCTOR: I think you need to go to the hospital so we can do some tests.

How long has it been _____ ⁹ you had a physical examination?

PATIENT: I haven't seen a doctor _____ ¹⁰ more than a year.

DOCTOR: Well, you certainly need a complete examination. You really should take better care of yourself.

J **LISTENING** 🔊

Listen and complete the sentences.

1. ⓐ last week.
   b. two days.

2. a. last weekend.
   b. three days.

3. a. Monday morning.
   b. more than a week.

4. a. a long time.
   b. I returned from my trip.

5. a. many weeks.
   b. we got married.

6. a. over a week.
   b. I started calling him.

7. a. the past few months.
   b. we discovered termites.

8. a. two or three weeks.
   b. I bought it.

9. a. at least a week.
   b. the other day.

K WHAT'S THE ANSWER?

1. I can't _____ my new apartment until next week.
   a. move into
   b. move

2. My husband almost always _____ the children after school.
   a. picks out
   b. picks up

3. My cousin said she would come over and _____ my new curtains.
   a. put on
   b. put up

4. Please tell Ms. Lee I'm _____, and I'll be at the office soon.
   a. on my way
   b. in my way

5. My husband and I have to _____ a gift for his sister's new baby.
   a. pick out
   b. pick on

6. It's important to _____ the application completely.
   a. fill
   b. fill out

7. Our teacher wants us to _____ the math problems by ourselves.
   a. figure
   b. figure out

8. Can you send someone to _____ my new computer?
   a. hook up
   b. hook on

9. I need some help this afternoon. Can you possibly _____?
   a. give me a hand
   b. hand me

10. Before I can use it, I need to _____ my new cell phone.
    a. call
    b. program

L COMPLETE THE SENTENCES

1. I'm sorry I can't help you move tomorrow. I have to work.

   If I _____didn't have to_____ work, I'd be glad to help you move.

2. It's a shame you're sick. If I had known you _____ sick, I wouldn't have bothered you.

3. I'm sorry you're having trouble _____ up your satellite dish. If I _____ busy all day, I'd be happy to help you.

4. I didn't realize you _____ programmed your new cell phone. That's why I couldn't reach you.

5. If I _____ on my way to an important job interview now, _____ be glad to help you hook up your new TV.

6. It's too bad you're having trouble _____ out the math problems. _____ come over and help you, but I've got a doctor's appointment.

7. If I _____ about _____ leave for a vacation, _____ be happy to help you move today.

8. I didn't know you _____ trouble setting up your computer. If I _____ you _____ trouble, I _____ come over and helped you. Next time you have a problem, don't forget to call me.

Listen. Then clap and practice.

If I had known   you were packing   for your trip   to Japan,

I never would have   called you   to help me   fix my van.

If I had known that   your children   were sick   with the flu,

I never would have   offered   to take them   to the zoo.

If I had known   you were waiting for   the carpenter   to call,

I never would have   asked you   to help me   paint my hall.

If I had known that   your relatives   were visiting   from Spain,

I never would have   called you   to help me   fix my drain.

If I had known that   you were planning   to give your dog   a bath,

I never would have   called you   to help me   with my math.

about	by	in	into	of	on	out	to	up	with

1. I can't stop sneezing. I think I'm allergic ___to___ something in this room!

2. Do you _____ any chance know when the movie begins?

3. Sylvia is being sent to London _____ business next month.

4. I got confused, and I mixed _____ the sugar and flour containers.

5. Jack got _____ a terrible argument, and I had to break up the fight.

6. If you drop _____ of school, I know you'll regret it.

7. What are you worried _____? I'm sure you'll do well on the exam.

8. The elevator in our building has been out _____ order for several weeks!

9. They don't have anything _____ common. Do they get along _____ each other?

about	at	by	from	in	of	off	on	past	to	up	with

10. I'll be away for a few days. I'm sorry I won't be able to help you hook _____ your new computer.

11. Do you by any chance know who this beautiful building was designed _____?

12. I'm not sure whether your car is ready. Why don't you check _____ the mechanic?

13. I'm concerned _____ Mrs. Wong. She was taken _____ the hospital last night.

14. The Blakes love their new apartment. It has a beautiful view _____ the river.

15. You've been complaining all day. You're _____ a terrible mood, aren't you!

16. I think you just drove _____ my house. We'll have to turn around.

17. Let's meet at Dave's Diner for lunch _____ around noon.

18. I should have turned _____ the TV and gone to sleep!

19. We ate lunch at a restaurant far _____ our office.

20. Careful! Don't step _____ that wet floor!

WHAT'S THE WORD?

allergic	ingredients	quit	tie
balance	mess	realize	tournament
delete	misunderstood	scrap	unemployed
files	move out	slipped	wallpaper
hamster	passport	suspect	wisdom

1. My father is wearing a cast on his leg. He lost his _____balance_____ and fell off a ladder.

2. Don't forget to take your _____ with you when you leave the country.

3. The painter says we need new _____ in our living room.

4. The police finally arrested the _____ in all the robberies in our neighborhood.

5. My son is growing up. Last week he learned how to _____ his shoes.

6. I'm sorry I missed your barbecue last week. It completely _____ my mind.

7. Edward couldn't finish making his cake. He ran out of _____.

8. Many people need to have their _____ teeth removed.

9. It's difficult for parents to adjust when their children grow up and _____ on their own.

10. The McDonalds had to get rid of their cat because Mr. McDonald was _____ to it.

11. It isn't a good idea to _____ your job if the economy isn't good.

12. My friends and I did our homework incorrectly. We must have _____ the directions.

13. Our _____ got out of its cage and made a big _____ in the kitchen.

14. Here. You can use this. It's just a piece of _____ paper.

15. I hope I find a job soon. I hate being _____.

16. Cindy is a talented athlete. She won the school tennis _____ again.

17. Do you _____ what you just did?!

18. Be careful! Don't hit the wrong key and _____ all the _____ on your computer.

P LISTENING

Read the questions. Listen to each passage. Then answer the questions.

Jeff's Problem

1. Jeff's friend advised him _____.
   a. not to talk to his boss
   (b.) to talk to his boss

2. Jeff told his boss _____.
   a. why he didn't like his job
   b. why he was satisfied with his work

3. Jeff's boss said _____.
   a. she complained too much
   b. she wasn't pleased with his work

4. Jeff wishes _____.
   a. he had listened to his friend
   b. he weren't unemployed

Amy and Tom

5. Amy's parents told her _____.
   a. to marry Tom
   b. not to marry Tom

6. Amy's parents thought Tom was _____.
   a. lazy
   b. successful

7. Amy is happy because _____.
   a. she followed her parents' advice
   b. Tom has been a wonderful husband

8. Amy isn't concerned because her sons _____.
   a. aren't like their father
   b. are just like her husband

Q OUT OF PLACE

1. cut	bite	(date)	hurt	destroy
2. superintendent	politician	mail carrier	snowman	librarian
3. CD	DVD	disk	mural	keyboard
4. astronomy	chemistry	apology	history	philosophy
5. lake	pond	ocean	poodle	river
6. teacher	baker	customer	professor	instructor
7. depressed	discovered	disappointed	upset	sick and tired
8. hamster	cockroach	cactus	dolphin	puppy
9. usher	prime minister	mayor	senator	governor
10. unemployed	fired	retired	promoted	out of work
11. assemble	delete	disconnect	erase	lose
12. amazing	fascinating	magnificent	aggressive	impressive
13. rewrite	register	replace	reopen	repaint
14. tires	accident	headlight	bumper	battery
15. annoyed	irritable	angry	mad	confused

Listen to each word and then say it.

1. b<u>l</u>ush—b<u>r</u>ush
2. <u>l</u>ight—<u>r</u>ight
3. long—w<u>r</u>ong
4. <u>v</u>ote—<u>b</u>oat
5. <u>ch</u>op—<u>sh</u>op
6. <u>sh</u>e's—<u>ch</u>eese
7. wat<u>ch</u>—wa<u>sh</u>
8. hear<u>d</u>—hur<u>t</u>
9. ri<u>d</u>e—wri<u>t</u>e
10. ri<u>dd</u>en—wri<u>tt</u>en
11. so<u>m</u>eday—Su<u>n</u>day
12. <u>m</u>ice—<u>n</u>ice
13. sen<u>d</u>—sen<u>t</u>
14. wi<u>d</u>e—whi<u>t</u>e
15. ru<u>n</u>—ru<u>ng</u>

S **HAVE YOU HEARD?**

Listen and complete the sentences.

watch   wash

1. a. . . . TV?
   b. . . . my shirt? It's dirty.

light   right

2. a. . . . I agree with you.
   b. . . . just went out. It's dark in here.

Someday   Sunday

3. a. . . . is my favorite day of the week.
   b. . . . I'll be rich and famous.

long   wrong

4. a. . . . It's more than 3 pages.
   b. . . . , but I can't find my mistake.

light   right

5. a. . . . I can lift it easily.
   b. . . . Your answer is fine.

watch   wash

6. a. . . . the dishes now.
   b. . . . my favorite TV program.

hurt   heard

7. a. . . . about Jane?
   b. . . . your arm?

chopping   shopping

8. a. . . . onions.
   b. . . . at the supermarket.

boys   voice

9. a. . . . are my nephews.
   b. . . . is better than mine.

heard   hurt

10. a. . . . my ankle.
    b. . . . from Jack recently.

ridden   written

11. a. . . . to your cousins?
    b. . . . your bicycle recently?

blushes   brushes

12. a. . . . when he makes a mistake.
    b. . . . his teeth every morning.

A.   Complete the sentences.

Ex. Betty was in the office yesterday, _____wasn't she_____ ?

1. The plane hasn't arrived yet, _____?

2. You fed the hamster, _____?

3. There weren't any cell phones when you were young, _____?

4. We don't need a new toaster, _____?

5. Your son plays on the school baseball team, _____?

6. Your parents won't be home this afternoon, _____?

7. You didn't forget to drop off the clothes at the cleaners, _____?

8. You can come to my party this weekend, _____?

9. I'm a good husband, _____?

10. You'll be finished soon, _____?

B.   Respond with an emphatic sentence.

Ex. A.   Howard is a hard worker.

   B.   You're right. _____He is a hard worker_____ , ____isn't he____!

1. A.   Aunt Fran hasn't called in a long time.

   B.   You're right. _____, _____!

2. A.   That was a boring movie.

   B.   I agree. _____, _____!

3. A.   Carol works very hard.

   B.   You're right. _____, _____!

4. A.   Your son will be a fine doctor someday.

   B.   I agree. _____, _____!

5. A.   Those cookies taste wonderful.

   B.   You're right. _____, _____!

C. Write the question.

Ex. I've decided to <u>quit my job</u>. _____What have you decided to do_____?

1. We'll be staying <u>at the Ritz Hotel</u>. _____?

2. We got engaged <u>a few days ago</u>. _____?

3. We spent <u>fifty dollars</u>. _____?

4. My father has been cooking <u>all day</u>. _____?

5. She mentioned you <u>six times</u>. _____?

6. I was assembling <u>my new bookcases</u>. _____?

7. He goes to the gym <u>because he wants to lose weight</u>. _____?

D. Fill in the blanks.

see

I don't really feel like _____¹ a movie again tonight. I usually enjoy _____²

movies, but I've already _____³ three movies this week, and I just _____⁴

a very boring movie last night. If I _____⁵ so many movies this week, I'd be happy

_____⁶ a movie with you tonight.

E. Listening

Listen and complete the sentences.

Ex. a. I never drive past your house.
  (b.) I never would have driven past your house.

1. a. I'd be happy to take a walk with you today.
   b. I'll be happy to take a walk with your today.

2. a. I wouldn't delete all my files.
   b. I wouldn't have deleted all my files.

3. a. if you go dancing all the time.
   b. if you went dancing all the time.

4. a. I wouldn't have called you.
   b. I won't call you.

5. a. I'll be glad to help you put in your air conditioner.
   b. I'd be glad to help you put in your air conditioner.

A TECHNOLOGY IN OUR LIVES

Read the article on student book page 159 and answer the questions.

1. In general, the article states that technology has _____ our lives.
   a. limited
   b. improved
   c. increased
   d. protected

2. The most changes in technology have come in the past _____.
   a. year
   b. 10 years
   c. 100 years
   d. 200 years

3. The first telephones didn't have any _____.
   a. receivers
   b. operators
   c. calls
   d. dials

4. Doctors use _____ to help people in remote areas.
   a. satellite communication
   b. scanners
   c. ATMs
   d. "smart highways"

5. Nowadays, a cashier can _____ to enter the price of an item.
   a. pay by credit card
   b. scan a bar code
   c. use a cell phone
   d. take a picture

6. Currently, people are NOT able to _____.
   a. use a "smart highway"
   b. send digital photos by e-mail
   c. do banking online
   d. use a store scanner without a cashier

7. The author's *structure* in paragraph 2 _____.
   a. compares current and future technology in our lives
   b. describes technology problems and solutions
   c. describes historical events in sequence (order)
   d. compares old and new technology in our lives

8. *Smart homes* in paragraph 3 means homes where computers _____.
   a. clean rooms
   b. destroy privacy
   c. control home appliances
   d. enter and leave rooms

9. In the last paragraph, *technology has its price* means _____.
   a. technology is expensive
   b. technology presents problems
   c. technology makes things cheaper
   d. technology for ATMs and banking is most important

10. You can infer from the last paragraph that the author's *point of view* is that _____.
    a. technology is always good
    b. lonely people like technology
    c. technology protects personal information
    d. protecting the privacy of information is important

B FACT FILE

Look at the Fact File on student book page 159 and answer the questions.

1. There were approximately _____ Internet users in 1996.
   a. 50
   b. 50,000
   c. 5,000,000
   d. 50,000,000

2. The number of Internet users increased by about _____ between 1995 and 2000.
   a. 40 million
   b. 200 million
   c. 280 million
   d. 320 million

C AROUND THE WORLD

Read the article on student book page 160 and answer the questions.

1. Many people use _____ to communicate with family members who live far away.
   a. video conferences
   b. scanners
   c. telemedicine
   d. e-mail

2. _____ are used to provide electricity in Sudan.
   a. Satellite dishes
   b. Solar batteries
   c. Utilities
   d. Scanners

3. In Japan, eye-scanning technology is used to _____ a person's identity.
   a. name
   b. ask about
   c. verify
   d. take a photo of

4. In many _____, scanners are used to screen luggage.
   a. airports
   b. hospitals
   c. homes
   d. stores

5. Telemedicine allows a doctor to _____ a patient.
   a. only talk with
   b. see and talk with
   c. talk with and touch
   d. do a blood test on

6. Many cars have _____ that allow drivers to see a map.
   a. video cameras
   b. keyboards
   c. computers
   d. scanners

7. In some remote areas, television service is received by a _____.
   a. DVD
   b. satellite dish
   c. cable system
   d. solar battery

8. Businesspeople from different locations can have a meeting using _____.
   a. a video conference
   b. a tape recorder
   c. telemedicine
   d. a meeting room

9. New technology is used _____.
   a. mostly by businesspeople
   b. only by residents in remote areas
   c. only for personal enjoyment
   d. by businesses and individuals

10. You can infer that technology makes distances between people seem _____.
    a. more important
    b. shorter
    c. longer
    d. more difficult

D YOU'RE THE INTERVIEWER!

Read the interviews on student book page 161. Then interview a classmate, a neighbor, or a friend. Use the chart below to record the person's answers. Share what you learned with the class.

How much time do you spend each day on a computer? a phone? a tablet or other device?	
Which technology do you use to keep in touch with your friends?	
What is your favorite type of technology? Why?	
How has technology changed your life in the last five years?	

Choose the best response.

1. Our computer must be out of memory.
   a. Yes. I forgot it.
   b. Let's turn it off.
   c. Yes. We have too much information on it.
   d. That's okay. We can telecommute.

2. Oh, no! My computer is frozen!
   a. Since nothing is happening, you should restart it.
   b. You can't use it when it's so cold.
   c. That's okay. It will just work slowly.
   d. My software doesn't work either.

3. Do you think my computer has a virus?
   a. Yes. You should call a doctor.
   b. Yes. None of the programs are working correctly.
   c. Yes. You need a new computer.
   d. Yes. It feels very warm.

4. I think this software has a bug.
   a. Look carefully. Can you see it?
   b. That software often has problems.
   c. It must be very old.
   d. That's because it doesn't have enough memory.

F WE'VE GOT MAIL!

Read the letters on student book page 162 and choose the correct answer.

1. It's a good idea to _____ English after finishing the *Side by Side* program.
   a. take a break from studying
   b. keep studying
   c. stop studying
   d. only study

2. Most students _____ grammar.
   a. should stop studying
   b. don't need to learn more
   c. should forget about
   d. should keep studying

3. Watching movies is a good way to _____.
   a. improve your English
   b. enjoy your classes
   c. communicate with people
   d. learn grammar rules

4. Studying in class and using English outside the classroom _____.
   a. have to be done with a teacher
   b. will confuse you
   c. are both important
   d. are very similar

G "CAN-DO" REVIEW

Match the "can do" statement and the correct sentence.

_____ 1. I can verify information.
_____ 2. I can congratulate someone.
_____ 3. I can initiate a topic of conversation.
_____ 4. I can ask for a reason.
_____ 5. I can invite someone to do something.
_____ 6. I can express feelings and emotions.
_____ 7. I can call attention to a person's actions.
_____ 8. I can apologize.
_____ 9. I can make a deduction.
_____ 10. I can express concern about someone.

a. You know . . .
b. Would you like to have lunch with me?
c. I must have pressed the wrong button.
d. Do you realize what you just did?
e. Congratulations!
f. I'm sorry.
g. You seem upset. Is anything wrong?
h. What makes you think I'm nervous?
i. It's going to rain today, isn't it?
j. I'm disappointed.

Listening Scripts

Page 3   Exercise C
Listen and decide what is being talked about.

1. A. Have they sung them yet?
   B. Yes, they have. They sang them a little while ago.
2. A. Has she written it yet?
   B. Yes, she has. She wrote it a little while ago.
3. A. I've spoken it for a long time.
   B. Oh. I didn't know that.
4. A. Have you swum there?
   B. Yes. We've swum there for a long time.
5. A. Have you ridden it yet?
   B. Yes. I rode it a little while ago.
6. A. I've drawn them for many years.
   B. I didn't know that.
7. A. Have you taken it?
   B. Yes, we have. We took it a little while ago.
8. A. Have you driven it yet?
   B. Yes. I drove it a little while ago.
9. A. She's grown them for many years.
   B. Yes. I knew that.

Page 6   Exercise G
Listen and complete the sentences.

1. A. How long have you played the violin?
   B. I've played the violin for . . .
2. A. How long has Peter known Monica?
   B. He's known her since . . .
3. A. How long have Mr. and Mrs. Johnson had that car?
   B. They've had it since . . .
4. A. How long have we been married?
   B. We've been married for . . .
5. A. How long has your sister had the flu?
   B. She's had the flu for . . .
6. A. How long have you wanted to be an actor?
   B. I've wanted to be an actor since . . .
7. A. How long has Debbie sung in the church choir?
   B. She's sung in the church choir since . . .
8. A. How long have you been a teacher?
   B. I've been a teacher for . . .
9. A. How long has Kevin had a Boston accent?
   B. He's had a Boston accent for . . .

Page 8   Exercise K
Listen and choose the correct answer.

1. I'm really frustrated. I've been having problems with my TV for the past few weeks, and I can't find anyone who can fix it.
2. I think I'll start looking for another job. I've been working here at the State Street Bank since I graduated from college.
3. We've been sitting here for more than a half hour, and no one has taken our order yet.
4. Do you think Peter and Jane will get married someday? After all, they've been going out since they were in high school.
5. We've been complaining to our landlord about the ceiling in our bedroom, but he hasn't done anything about it. We don't know what to do. It's been leaking for the past two weeks.
6. I'm exhausted. We've been riding around town all day. Let's stop somewhere and rest for a while.

Page 29   Exercise M
Listen and choose the correct answer.

1. Billy fell asleep in school today.
2. Alice called her friends at midnight and woke them up.
3. I wonder why Gary didn't come to the meeting this morning.
4. We sat at the football game in the rain all afternoon.
5. Roger was hoping to get a promotion this year, but he didn't get one.
6. The play was terrible. The actors couldn't remember their lines!
7. I called my cousin Betty all week, but she didn't answer the phone.
8. Grandpa moved the refrigerator by himself!

Page 31   Exercise P: *Have You Heard?*
Listen and complete the sentences.

1. How do you feel . . .
2. Do you still . . .
3. Does he like these . . .
4. She needed . . .
5. They live . . .
6. We're leaving . . .
7. Alan is sleeping late because he's . . .
8. I'm sorry you didn't like the salad. It . . .
9. I'll try to finish this . . .
10. This week . . .
11. Will you still want to see your old friends when you're rich . . .
12. You should fill . . .
13. They don't feed . . .
14. I'm glad you like the chocolate cake. Eat . . .
15. I don't think those boys steal . . .
16. George is very glad his . . .

Page 35   Exercise E
Listen and decide what is being talked about.

1. They've already been made.
2. It was directed by Fellini.
3. It was sent last week.
4. It was worn by her grandmother.
5. They've already been given out.
6. They've already been written.
7. It's already been sung.
8. They've already been fed.
9. It's already been set up.

Page 39   Exercise L
Listen and choose the correct answer.

1. Hello. This is Mrs. Riley. I'm calling about my VCR. Is it ready?
2. Is the meeting room ready?
3. This is a beautiful photograph of your children.
4. I can't wait to hear those songs.
5. Why is Robert so upset?
6. We've been waiting all morning for the courier from your company.
7. Have you heard the good news about Nancy's raise?
8. Why is Roberta so pleased?
9. Where are the new pictures we bought last weekend?
10. Is the birthday cake ready?
11. I'm really looking forward to hearing the Mozart sonata.
12. Why is Aunt Helen so happy?

Page 43   Exercise R
Listen and choose the correct answer.

1. This magnificent mural is being painted by students in our school.
2. Mrs. Allen, your watch has been repaired.
3. The beds will be done soon.
4. All the paychecks have been given out.
5. The meeting room is ready now.

(continued)

6. Mr. Winter, your car is being repaired.
7. All the cookies have been baked.
8. The babies are being fed.

Page 45   Exercise D
Listen and choose the correct answer.
Ex: It's already been painted.
1. All the photographs have been taken.
2. The holiday decorations are being hung up.
3. The beds on the third floor are ready now.
4. The report is being rewritten right now.
5. Mr. Williams, your VCR has been repaired.

Page 49   Exercise E
Listen and decide what is being talked about.
1. I'm sorry. I don't know what time it arrives. Check with the ticket agent.
2. I have no idea what this means.
3. Do you have any idea when this was taken?
4. I have no idea what the problem is with the engine. Check with the mechanic.
5. I have no idea what time it begins. You should look in the newspaper.
6. I'm sorry. I don't know how much this costs. You should ask that salesperson over there.
7. Do you know when they were sent?
8. Do you have any idea when they were fed?

Page 53   Exercise J
Listen and decide where these people are.
1. Can you tell me if surfing is allowed here?
2. Do you by any chance know whether these shirts are on sale?
3. Do you know whether the play has begun yet?
4. Do you remember if our car is on the third floor or on the fourth?
5. Do you have any idea if it'll be arriving soon?
6. Could you tell me whether there's a lot of pepper in the stew?
7. Do you know whether swimming is allowed here?
8. Could you possibly tell me if lettuce is on sale this week?
9. Do you by any chance know if the monkeys are sleeping?

Page 58   Exercise D
Listen and complete the sentences.
1. If it rains this weekend, . . .
2. I'll skip dessert if . . .
3. We'll be late for work if . . .
4. If they finish their homework soon, . . .
5. If our car doesn't start tomorrow morning, . . .
6. If you don't come to class next Monday, . . .
7. I know I'll fall asleep in class if . . .
8. I'll send your package by overnight mail if . . .
9. If Charlie doesn't get a raise soon, . . .
10. Please call me if . . .
11. Janet will pick up her husband at the airport if . . .
12. If the children don't feel any better, . . .
13. We won't go on vacation if . . .
14. She'll regret it if . . .

Page 63   Exercise J
Listen and choose the polite response.
1. Do you think it will snow soon so we can go skiing?
2. Do you think you'll lose your job?
3. Will the teacher yell at us if we make a mistake?
4. Do you think the baby will cry all night?
5. Will Jane go out with me if I ask her?
6. Am I going to regret taking this job?
7. Am I going to have trouble on my history exam?
8. Will you graduate soon?
9. Will the movie be exciting?

10. Will there be pickpockets in the crowd?
11. Do you think John will apologize to his sister?
12. Will YOUR children give their colds to MY children?

Page 66   Exercise N
Listen and choose the correct answer based on what you hear.
1. You know, George, if you took more vacations, you'd feel more energetic.
2. I would enjoy listening to the orchestra if the musicians were more talented.
3. If you were more aggressive, you'd be a much better used car salesman.
4. Bob's car would be in better condition if he tuned it up more often.
5. If they had more in common, they'd get along with each other.
6. If Mona were a good teacher, she'd care more about her students.
7. We would be able to use the Internet if our school had more computers.
8. If these cookies had more sugar, they'd be sweeter.

Page 77   Exercise D
Listen and complete the sentences.
Ex. If the weather is nice this weekend, . . .
1. If I miss the bus, . . .
2. If I were more careful, . . .
3. You'll regret it if . . .
4. If I didn't have to work overtime, . . .
5. If she weren't busy this weekend, . . .

Page 80   Exercise E
Listen and complete the sentences.
1. I wouldn't grow a beard if I were you. If you grew a beard, . . .
2. I'm not feeling well today, but if I feel better tomorrow, . . .
3. You know, I wouldn't ride in that old car if I were you. If you rode in that old car, . . .
4. If I have some time this weekend, . . .
5. I wouldn't show this political cartoon to the president. If you showed it to him, . . .
6. To be honest, I wouldn't go to Alaska in February. If you went there in February, . . .
7. If I have to spend a lot of money on car repairs this year, . . .
8. If I were you, I wouldn't buy a used computer. If you bought a used computer, . . .
9. If you skip today's meeting, I know . . .
10. To be honest with you, I wouldn't start an Internet company if I were you. If you did, . . .
11. If you keep on parking your car in my parking space, . . .
12. To tell the truth, I wouldn't marry George if I were you. If you married him, . . .

Page 83   Exercise I
Listen and complete the conversations.
1. A. Do you think the weather in London is sunny and warm at this time of year?
   B. No, I don't. But I wish . . .
2. A. Are you unhappy when I talk too much?
   B. Yes, I am. I wish . . .
3. A. Does your daughter enjoy her English class?
   B. Yes, she does. But she wishes . . .
4. A. Do you think Michael daydreams too much in class?
   B. Yes, I do. I wish . . .
5. A. Do you like scary movies?
   B. Yes. As a matter of fact, I usually wish . . .

6. A. Are you annoyed when I sing loudly in the shower?
   B. The truth is, I wish . . .
7. A. Do you like your cell phone?
   B. Yes, I do. But I wish . . .
8. A. Are you tired of getting stuck in traffic?
   B. Of course, I am. I wish . . .
9. A. Do you like being single?
   B. It's okay. But the truth is, I wish . . .
10. A. Are you enjoying living in your new apartment?
    B. It's fine, but it's a little too small. I wish . . .
11. A. Is Harry upset about being laid off?
    B. He certainly is. He wishes . . .
12. A. Are you worried when I don't call you?
    B. Yes, I am. I wish . . .

Page 86 Exercise N
Listen and decide what the person is talking about.

1. If your pronunciation were better, I'd be able to understand you.
2. If I planted them now, I could eat them in three months.
3. If I took driver's ed, I could get it soon.
4. If I skipped it, my mother would be angry.
5. If I saved enough, I'd probably be able to visit you.
6. If I didn't concentrate, I could make a mistake.

Page 93 Exercise E
Listen and choose the statement that is true based on what you hear.

1. If she had spoken more confidently at her job interview, she would have gotten the job.
2. If he hadn't been late for work every day, he wouldn't have gotten fired.
3. If it had rained, we would have had to cancel the picnic.
4. If you hadn't been in a hurry, you wouldn't have made so many careless mistakes on your homework.
5. If I had remembered their phone number, I would have called them.
6. If the play hadn't been so boring, the audience wouldn't have fallen asleep.
7. If we had been in the mood to go swimming, we would have gone to the beach with you.
8. If he hadn't been speeding, he wouldn't have gotten a ticket.
9. If I had written legibly, they would have been able to read my letter.
10. If I hadn't forgotten about the meeting, I definitely would have been there.

Page 102 Exercise R
Listen and complete the sentences.

1. I wish I didn't have an exam tomorrow. If I didn't have an exam, . . .
2. I hope we're having spaghetti for dinner tonight. If we're having spaghetti for dinner, . . .
3. I wish my brother weren't in a bad mood all the time. If he weren't in a bad mood all the time, . . .
4. I wish my daughter had taken her umbrella to school. If she had taken her umbrella, . . .
5. I hope Jim is at the party Saturday night. If he's at the party, . . .
6. I wish I lived near a bus stop. If I lived near a bus stop, . . .

Page 102 Exercise S: *Hopes and Wishes*
Listen and complete the sentences.

1. My son isn't feeling very well. I wish . . .
2. I was confused about yesterday's English lesson. I hope . . .
3. My best friend just moved away. I wish . . .

4. Alice hates working at Paul's Pizza Shop. She hopes . . .
5. I sometimes feel lonely. I wish . . .
6. I'll try not to step on your feet. I wish . . .
7. The school play is this weekend. We hope . . .
8. My daughter lost her notebook. I wish . . .
9. I'm making chocolate chip cookies for dessert. I hope . . .
10. This cactus looks terrible. I wish . . .
11. Our fax machine is broken. I hope . . .
12. Vicky's used car has been giving her a lot of trouble. She wishes . . .
13. I don't have any eggs. I hope . . .
14. I sometimes forget people's names. I wish . . .

Page 103 Exercise U: *Have You Heard?*
Listen and complete the sentences.

1. This morning I met . . .
2. They fell . . .
3. A tailor . . .
4. There isn't enough pepper . . .
5. Are you afraid . . .
6. Have they made . . .
7. The men . . .
8. We're going to shake . . .
9. My daughter's wedding . . .
10. Nancy's neighbor . . .
11. Barbara paid . . .
12. I'll check . . .
13. I don't want to go to school because I fail . . .
14. We have to hurry because Tom's waiting . . .
15. Roger's never . . .
16. I'm Fred . . .

Page 108 Exercise E
What did they say? Listen and choose the correct answer.

1. I have some good news. I can fix your car next week.
2. My daughter is going to have a baby in July.
3. I have an important announcement. Tomorrow's meeting has been canceled.
4. My wife was just promoted to manager of her department.
5. I don't believe it! The bus drivers are going on strike!
6. I love Melanie, and she loves me!
7. You won't believe it! The monkeys have escaped from the zoo!
8. I'm nervous about my interview tomorrow.
9. My parents sold their house and moved into a condominium.
10. I'm going to do something I've always wanted to do. I'm going to quit my job and move to Hollywood!

Page 110 Exercise H
Listen and choose the correct answer.

1. Patty, did you break up with Gary?
2. How long have you been sitting here?
3. Were you reading when they called?
4. When are you going to repaint it?
5. Are you still mad?
6. When are you going to study math?
7. Are they too small?
8. Who fixed the kitchen floor?

Page 123 Exercise D
Listen and complete the sentences.

Ex: I wish I didn't have to study tonight. If I didn't have to study tonight, . . .

1. I wish I hadn't been sick last weekend. If I hadn't been sick, . . .
2. I wish I were an optimist. If I were an optimist, . . .
3. The landlord called this morning. He said . . .

(continued)

4. You won't believe what my girlfriend asked me! She asked me . . .
5. You won't believe what one of my students asked me! He asked me . . .

Page 129   Exercise G
Listen and complete the sentences.
1. You live at the corner of Broadway and Main, . . .
2. You aren't thinking of quitting, . . .
3. We don't need any more onions, . . .
4. You returned your library books, . . .
5. Nancy doesn't go out with Peter any more, . . .
6. You've done your assignment, . . .
7. Your sister was invited to the wedding, . . .
8. He's been a good employee, . . .
9. We won't we leaving soon, . . .
10. My brother and I can swim at this beach, . . .
11. This isn't your parking space, . . .
12. I didn't forget to call my mother last weekend, . . .

Page 132   Exercise L
Listen and complete the conversations.
1. A. Ruth is going to be a doctor, isn't she?
   B. Actually, she isn't.
   A. She isn't?! That's surprising! I was sure . . .
2. A. You sold your house, didn't you?
   B. Actually, I didn't.
   A. You didn't?! I'm surprised. I was sure . . .
3. A. This car has new brakes, doesn't it?
   B. No, it doesn't.
   A. It doesn't?! I was sure . . .
4. A. You aren't angry with me, are you?
   B. Actually, I am.
   A. You are?! I'm disappointed. I was sure . . .
5. A. Your cousins from Chicago will be arriving this weekend, won't they?
   B. Actually, they won't be arriving until next month.
   A. Oh. I was sure . . .
6. A. You didn't get searched at the airport, did you?
   B. Actually, I did.
   A. You did?! I'm surprised. I was sure . . .
7. A. Children aren't allowed to see this movie, are they?
   B. Actually, they are.
   A. They are?! That's very surprising! I was sure . . .
8. A. Albert still works at the bank, doesn't he?
   B. Actually, he doesn't.
   A. He doesn't?! I didn't know that. I was sure . . .
9. A. Cynthia was hired by the Bay Company, wasn't she?
   B. Actually, she wasn't.
   A. She wasn't?! That's too bad. I was sure . . .
10. A. Dr. Miller can deliver babies, can't he?
    B. Actually, he can't. He's a dentist.
    A. Oh. I didn't know that. I was sure . . .

Page 145   Exercise J
Listen and complete the sentences.
1. My fax machine has been broken since . . .
2. My son has had chicken pox for . . .
3. Our elevator has been out of order since . . .
4. My passport has been missing since . . .
5. We've been having trouble communicating for . . .
6. He's refused to fix our shower for . . .
7. We've wanted to sell our house since . . .
8. I've been having problems with my VCR for . . .
9. My wisdom teeth have hurt since . . .

Page 150   Exercise P
Read the questions. Listen to each passage. Then answer the questions.

Jeff's Problem
When I was unhappy with my job last month, my friend told me not to complain to him. He said I should tell my boss how I felt. So I decided to take my friend's advice. I made an appointment with my boss and told her why I didn't like my job. My boss listened quietly for a while, and then she told me why she wasn't satisfied with my work. She said I worked much too slowly, I made too many mistakes, and I complained too much. She told me she thought we'd both be happier if I worked someplace else. I'm very sorry I listened to my friend's advice. If I hadn't listened to his advice, I wouldn't have been fired and I wouldn't be out of work right now.

Amy and Tom
I started going out with Tom when I was a teenager. We fell in love with each other when we were in high school. When I was 25 years old, Tom asked me to marry him, and I accepted. My parents urged me not to marry Tom. They told me if I married Tom, I'd always regret it. They said he didn't work hard enough, he wasn't serious enough, and he would never be successful. Well, I'm glad I didn't follow my parents' advice, and so are they. Tom and I have been married for 20 years, and we've been very happy. Tom has a good job, and he's a wonderful husband and father. Our sons are teenagers now, and my parents are a little concerned about them because they aren't serious enough. But I'm not worried about my sons at all. They're just like their father used to be.

Page 151   Exercise S: *Have You Heard?*
Listen and complete the sentences.
1. When are you going to wash . . .
2. You're right.
3. Someday . . .
4. My answer is long.
5. That's light.
6. It's time to watch . . .
7. Have you hurt . . .
8. I hate chopping . . .
9. My brother's voice . . .
10. I've heard . . .
11. Why haven't you written . . .
12. Alexander brushes . . .

Page 153   Exercise E
Listen and complete the sentences.
Ex. I'm sorry I drove past your house. I must have had my mind on something else. If I hadn't had my mind on something else, . . .
1. If I hadn't taken a walk yesterday, . . .
2. I can't believe I deleted all my files. I must have hit the wrong key. If I hadn't hit the wrong key, . . .
3. I'm sure you'd get tired of going dancing . . .
4. If I had known your relatives were visiting, . . .
5. If I weren't on my way to a concert, . . .